TITANIC

AN ILLUSTRATED HISTORY

WHITE STAR LINE

NAME _____ ROOM _____

BOOKED TO _____ VIA _____

STEAMER _____ SAILING _____

FULL FOREIGN ADDRESS _____

J-3487

WANTED
FIRST
CLASS

A WELLFLEET PRESS / MADISON PRESS BOOK

WELLFLEET
PRESS

TITANIC
AN ILLUSTRATED HISTORY

TEXT BY DON LYNCH ~ PAINTINGS BY KEN MARSCHALL

INTRODUCTION BY ROBERT D. BALLARD

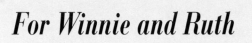

For Winnie and Ruth

This edition published in 2006 by
WELLFLEET PRESS
A division of BOOK SALES, INC.
114 Northfield Avenue
Edison, New Jersey 08837
USA

ISBN-13: 978-0-7858-1972-1

ISBN-10: 0-7858-1972-X

(Page 1)
A White Star luggage tag of the kind used on the Titanic.

(Page 3)
Having raised anchor for the last time off Queenstown, Ireland, the Titanic *passes Kinsale Head on April 11, 1912.*

(Pages 4–5)
In a scene similar to the Titanic's *departure, her sister ship, the* Olympic, *leaves Southampton.*

(Pages 6–7)
The giant hull is made ready for launching at the Belfast shipyards of Harland and Wolff.

(Page 8)
The liner picks up speed on the North Atlantic.

(Pages 10–11)
In their only encounter at sea, the Titanic *passes her sister ship, the* Olympic, *off Portland on the evening of April 3, 1912. En route from Belfast following her trails, the* Titanic *would dock in Southampton that midnight and begin preparations for her maiden voyage.*

(Page 12)
From their tiny submarine, Alvin, *Robert Ballard and two members of his team illuminate the fallen foremast of the* Titanic *wreck.*

(Pages 14–15)
Spectators approach the shipyard on the Titanic's *launch day.*

Produced by
Madison Press Books
1000 Yonge Street, Suite 200, Toronto, Ontario, Canada M4W 2K2

Printed in Singapore

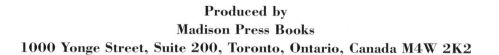

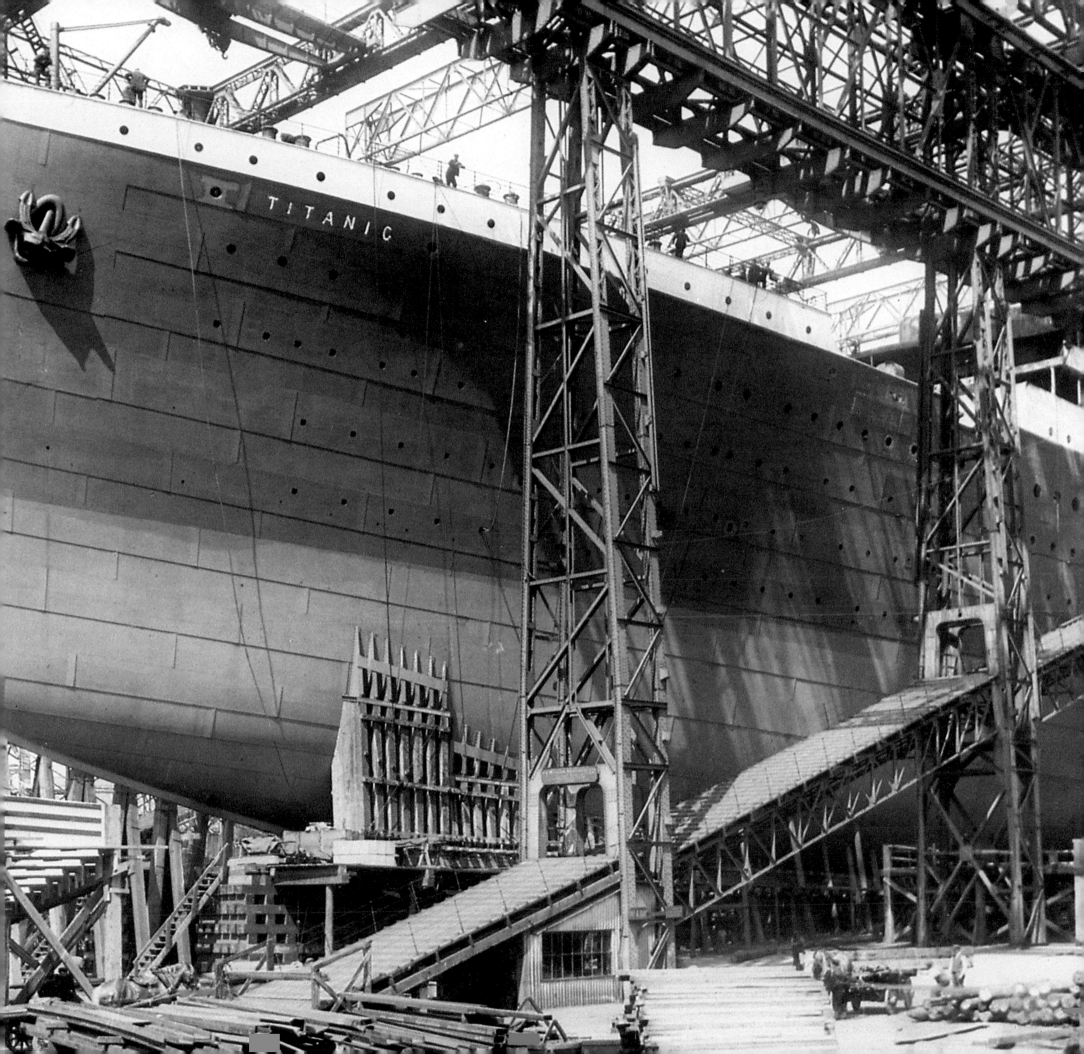

CONTENTS

INTRODUCTION

WHEN I FIRST THOUGHT ABOUT LOOKING FOR THE *Titanic*, the ship represented little more than a technological challenge: a famous wreck lost in deep water that would test the limits of the underwater robots I was developing for deep-sea research and exploration. However, the more familiar I became with her story, the more my fascination grew. Soon this grand old lady of the deep had me completely in her spell. But I have to admit even I was surprised at the overwhelming public response when we found the ship in 1985. After all, the *Titanic* went down in April 1912, eighty years ago. By all rights she should have been dead and buried long since. Yet her allure seems greater today than ever.

I've described the wreck of the *Titanic* as an entrancing deep-sea museum, and argued strongly that it be left unmolested by treasure seekers. Unfortunately, it's a museum few people will ever have the chance to visit. All the more reason then to welcome this extraordinary book, which combines what our and subsequent expeditions have learned about the wreck with the most complete compendium of *Titanic* lore ever gathered between hard covers. This book is a living museum you'll want to visit time and again. In it you will meet not only the rich and famous — the Astors and the Wideners and the Strauses — but many of the ordinary passengers whose lives were changed or ended by the *Titanic*'s maiden voyage.

Don Lynch, the historian of the Titanic Historical Society, has spent many years researching every aspect of the story. His fascinating text provides new insights into the voyage, the passengers, and crew. As Lynch writes, "part of the lure and mystery of the *Titanic* will always be its unanswered questions. Would a different captain have avoided the iceberg? Could the ship have been prevented from sinking? What kind of a hole did the iceberg cause in the hull? Ironically, the finding of the wreck in 1985 solved some of the mysteries, but it created others. More than anything, the discovery proved that the *Titanic* has become a permanent object of fascination for millions." I couldn't agree more.

It gives me particular pleasure to salute the amazing artistic skills of Ken Marschall, whose contribution alone would make this book a collector's item. One day in July of 1986, after an exhausting dive to the *Titanic* wreck in our submersible *Alvin*, I was called to the bridge to take a call over satellite from *Time* magazine. The editors at *Time* wanted to feature our expedition on their cover, but in order to make their publishing deadline they wanted me to cut short my exploration of the ship to bring the images collected so far to their artist. I politely told them that this was out of the question and returned to our photographic work. The next day I received a second call from *Time*. They had changed their minds: if I would describe what I'd seen so far to their artist over the radio, they would go ahead with the cover story. I agreed, but inwardly I wondered how even the best artist in the world could come close to capturing the wreck I'd seen only in fragments, like pieces of a jigsaw puzzle.

Several days later I was back in Woods Hole, Massachusetts, and on my way to the lecture hall for a quick press conference when someone handed me a copy of *Time*. It stopped me in my tracks. There on the cover was the *Titanic*. Not someone's idea of what it might look like but a dead ringer of the ship I had been crawling over for two weeks in a cramped little sub with a flashlight. It was an image I'd carried around in my head but found impossible to describe to others. Yet Ken Marschall had captured that image for the rest of the world to see. If he could paint such an amazing portrait based on a quick description over a ship's radio, you can imagine what he has done after studying the thousands of images we collected.

I'll never forget my first good look at the *Titanic*. This was on our second dive in *Alvin* in 1986. Our headlights cut a narrow swath through the submarine darkness, illuminating nothing but gray mud. Suddenly a huge black shape loomed up out of the gloom, the knife-edge of the bow plowing the bottom into a gigantic wave as it came straight for us.... Later we would land on the boat deck, send *Jason Junior* down the Grand Staircase, and explore the vast debris field, but that moment will always stay with me, that image of the *Titanic* alive again.

In *Titanic: An Illustrated History*, the great lost liner is brought magnificently back to life. For those of you who can't visit the *Titanic* in person, this beautiful book is the next best thing.

Robert D. Ballard
Woods Hole, Massachusetts
January 1992

Chapter One

BUILDING THE LEGEND

London, England, 1907

ON A STILL, SUMMER EVENING IN 1907 a large Mercedes limousine pulled to a stop before an impressive white, porticoed residence in London's fashionable Belgravia district. A liveried chauffeur stepped from the open front seat of the vehicle and opened the door to the enclosed passenger compartment. A very tall man, dressed in evening clothes but wearing neither hat nor overcoat, emerged from the automobile and offered his arm to his wife, who was wearing a dark evening gown, to escort her into the house.

The elegantly attired man was J. Bruce Ismay, managing director of the White Star Line — a position he had negotiated when selling the firm, founded by his father, to the American financier J. Pierpont Morgan. The Belgravia mansion, known as Downshire House, was the home of Lord James Pirrie, a partner in the firm of Harland and Wolff, the giant Belfast shipbuilder that built all White Star vessels. Ismay and Pirrie were allies in a fierce fight for mastery of the lucrative Atlantic passenger trade, a competition in which their chief rival was Britain's venerable Cunard Line.

Dining with the Pirries could be a disconcerting experience. Lord Pirrie suffered from the cold and would sit at one end of the long table with a warm rug wrapped around his legs. At the opposite end Lady Pirrie would sit vigorously fanning herself, complaining to whomever sat beside her about the heat.

But Bruce Ismay was accustomed to his hosts' eccentricities. He and his wife Florence had dined at Downshire House often, and they likely did not comment on the temperature either way. On this night, however, the conversation fell to a more serious topic. The new Cunard liner, *Lusitania*, was on the minds of everyone in the maritime industry. The huge passenger ship was about to make her maiden voyage. Everyone expected her to shatter the existing speed record for an Atlantic crossing and put Cunard firmly ahead in the escalating race of the Atlantic superliners. How was White Star to counter the *Lusitania* and her sister ship, the *Mauretania*, then nearing completion?

During this dinner party, it is generally believed, Pirrie and Ismay hatched a daring plan. They would build two huge liners, with a third to follow. Each would be fifty percent larger than the *Lusitania*'s 30,000 gross tons, and nearly 100 feet longer than her 790 feet — so long that neither Harland and Wolff nor any other shipyard had a dry dock, crane, or gantry large enough to construct them. Luxury and comfort rather than speed would be their attraction, although the ships would be fast enough to make the crossing from England to New York in a week's time. In fact, by providing good rather than great speed, the vibration from

Lord and Lady Pirrie (top) in front of their Belfast home. He poses in the full regalia of an Irish Privy Councillor.
J. Bruce Ismay (above), managing director of the White Star Line.
(Left) The cover of a 1906 White Star passenger list.
Downshire House (right), the Pirries' London home, is where the idea for the Titanic *was born. Today it houses Spain's embassy to Great Britain.*

CUNARD LINE
LIVERPOOL
TO
NEW YORK & BOSTON

R.M.S. LUSITANIA
FIRST CLASS
DINING SALOON

The impetus to build the Titanic *was provided by the Cunard liner* Lusitania *(below) which was not only fast but luxurious as well. Her splendid first-class dining saloon (left) rivaled the best of Europe's hotels.*

The Lusitania's *sister ship, the* Mauretania *(above), served Cunard for twenty-nine years, during twenty-two of which she was the fastest liner in the world.*

the engines would be reduced, further enhancing the passengers' comfort.

Later that evening, after the cigars had been smoked and the port drunk, the patiently waiting chauffeur assisted Bruce and Florence Ismay into their limousine. As they drove home through the warm London night, one can imagine Ismay visualizing the triumphant entry of his new superships into the Atlantic contest — ships whose success would finally bring him out of his father's shadow.

The race for the Atlantic passenger trade actually began when Bruce Ismay's father, Thomas Henry Ismay, formed the White Star Line in 1869. Until then Cunard had been virtually unchallenged as the ruler of the Atlantic waves. A mere four years later, in 1873, the sixth White Star liner, the *Baltic*, set the eastbound Atlantic speed record and took the lead. For the next twenty years, despite the wreck of White Star's *Atlantic* in April 1873, the upstart company continued to rival and often surpass Cunard. First one and then the other gained the edge by introducing the latest technological advance. In 1889, with the launch of the *Teutonic* and *Majestic*, White Star introduced the modern ocean liner — a ship without sails, leaving its decks spacious and uncluttered. Soon luxury and size became more important than speed alone.

In the 1890s the Germans entered the race, and the competition became even more fierce. By the turn of the century growing immigration to North America and the larger numbers of wealthy travelers had increased the commercial potential of the passenger trade to such an extent that it drew the interest of the great American financier,

J. Pierpont Morgan. He began buying up shipping companies to form a trust operating under the name International Mercantile Marine. In 1902 he added White Star to create a consortium large enough to crush Cunard and the Germans. Bruce Ismay, as well as retaining the directorship of the White Star Line, was made chairman and managing director of IMM, but he technically worked for Morgan. It was Morgan's money that would bankroll Ismay's and Pirrie's dream to build three ships larger and more luxurious than any the world had seen.

Pirrie and Ismay acted quickly to move the idea for their superliners from dream to drawing board. Pirrie's staff worked to create a prac-

J. Pierpont Morgan (left) used some of his enormous wealth, parodied in a cartoon of the period (above), to gain control of the White Star Line.

ticable design while the Harland and Wolff shipyard in Belfast began converting three berths (where some of the world's biggest ships had been built) into two. A 220-foot-high gantry, the largest in the world, was to be constructed over the slips. Meanwhile, Ismay began negotiations with the New York Harbor Board, which had no pier long enough to accommodate the new vessels.

Originally the ships were to be three-funneled, but Pirrie felt four would give them better lines, so four it became. Compared to passenger ships of the time, the initial plans were in some ways simple and in others grandiose. First class had a rather ordinary stairwell, a huge lounge, a large reception room, a smoking room, reading room and two palm courts. The huge first-class dining room was three decks high and topped by a dome. Two elevators would ferry first-class passengers between the decks, and low in the ship an enormous spa the size of the first-class dining saloon boasted Turkish baths, swimming pool and gymnasium. Inevitably some of these features were scaled down or eliminated, and others were enhanced. The dome over the main dining room was replaced by a conventional ceiling; the spa was reduced in size and the gymnasium was moved to the top deck. The staircase was enlarged to fan out at the landing of each deck, with elaborate balustrades and a huge glass dome overhead. Two more elevators were added, yielding a total of three for first class and, another first, one for the use of second-class passengers.

Men of Iron by Belfast artist William Conor depicts a ship being prepared for launching in the same gantry that housed the Olympic *and the* Titanic.

FINALLY THE PLANS AND PREPARATIONS were complete. On December 16, 1908, over a year after the fateful dinner at Downshire House, the first keel plate was laid for a giant liner that would be called the *Olympic*. Three months later, on March 31, 1909, the first keel plate was laid for the *Titanic*.

While the two ships took shape in Belfast, the nagging problem of pier space in New York had yet to be resolved. Initially the New York Harbor Board refused to grant International Mercantile Marine permission to lengthen the White Star piers to accommodate the new liners. But New York's business community recognized the benefits these larger ships would bring, and represen-

BUILDING A LEVIATHAN

Architects and draftsmen (left) at Harland and Wolff worked in an enormous hall with a high barrel ceiling and huge windows that provided a maximum amount of natural light. The two ships stand side by side in the stocks (right) on the day the Olympic *was launched. The* Titanic *would follow seven months later. (Left) Some of Harland and Wolff's 14,000 employees stream down Queen's Road at the end of a long work day in May, 1911.*

A team of twenty horses (left) pulls a fifteen-and-a-half-ton anchor made for the Titanic. *Her hull completed, the* Titanic *awaits launch day (below).*

Ismay and Lord Pirrie (above) inspect the Titanic's *hull just prior to her launch .*
(Left) A view from the top of the gantry of the Olympic's *double bottom under construction.*

21

tatives were sent to Washington, D.C., to press the issue with the War Department, which had ultimate control over the harbor. Eventually IMM was given permission to extend the piers.

On October 20, 1910, the *Olympic* was launched and towed to her fitting-out basin for completion. Then, on May 31, 1911, J. P. Morgan, Bruce Ismay and his daughter Margaret, Lord

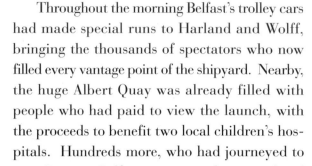
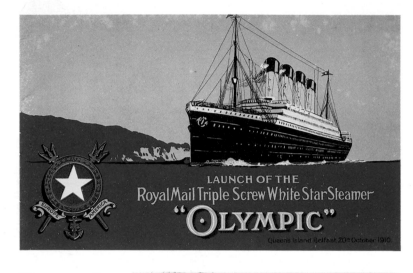

The cover of a brochure celebrating the Olympic's launch (above) and (right) a photograph of the event.

and Lady Pirrie, the Lord Mayor of Belfast, and numerous other dignitaries stood on a crimson-and-white-draped grandstand at the Harland and Wolff shipyard. Before them rose the port side of the *Titanic*, her nearly 26,000-ton hull freshly painted black. At the bow stood three more grandstands — two for ticketholders and another for over one hundred members of the press, most of whom had arrived on the steamer *Duke of Argyll*, which had been specially chartered by the White Star Line to bring them to Belfast from England.

Throughout the morning Belfast's trolley cars had made special runs to Harland and Wolff, bringing the thousands of spectators who now filled every vantage point of the shipyard. Nearby, the huge Albert Quay was already filled with people who had paid to view the launch, with the proceeds to benefit two local children's hospitals. Hundreds more, who had journeyed to Belfast to witness the event, lined the sides of the River Lagan, which had been dredged to accommodate the nearly thirty-five-foot draft of the *Olympic* and *Titanic*. Although the two ships were almost identical in size the *Titanic* was 1004 gross tons larger and would be in several ways more luxurious in her appointments.

As was the custom for White Star and Harland and Wolff, there was no christening. At 12:05 two rockets were fired, followed by a third five minutes later. At 12:13 the hull began to move under its own weight down the ways. Workmen on board waved their caps, and the thousands of spectators cheered. Tugs blew whistles and women waved handkerchiefs while the *Titanic* traveled twice her nearly nine-hundred-foot length, achieving twelve knots, before being brought to a halt by six anchor chains and two piles of cable drag chains weighing eighty tons each.

That same day Harland and Wolff proudly handed over the newly completed *Olympic* to the White Star Line, and for several hours the two ships could be seen floating in the same harbor. At 3:00 P.M. Morgan, Ismay, and the other dignitaries sailed for Liverpool aboard the *Olympic*. A new chapter in the race for the Atlantic passenger trade had begun.

It required twenty-three tons of tallow, train oil, and soft soap to grease the ways, as the Titanic was launched (above). She developed enormous momentum before the anchors and drag chains brought her to a stop in Belfast Harbour (far right). The whole process took only sixty-two seconds. Those fortunate enough to have obtained a launch ticket (right) were able to get a ringside view from within the gantry (middle right).

Launch
OF
White Star Royal Mail Triple-Screw Steamer
"TITANIC"
At BELFAST,
Wednesday, 31st May, 1911, at 12-15 p.m.

Admit Bearer.

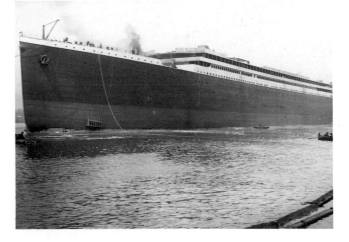

FITTING OUT

From empty hull to the most luxurious ocean liner afloat, the installation of machinery and the completion of the Titanic's *interiors took ten months and several million man-hours. Her first stop was the fitting-out basin (below). On February 3, 1912, she was dry-docked in the Belfast Harbour Commission's new graving dock (right) where her propellers were fitted and a final coat of paint applied.*

Some of the men who built the ships pose alongside the Olympic's *hull (above). At the beginning of March the* Olympic *briefly joined her sister, having returned to dry dock for the replacement of a propeller blade (right). This 1912 painting (left) by Charles Dixon is titled* The Titanic Being Fitted Out at Queen's Island, Belfast.

(Overleaf) On April 2, 1912, the completed Titanic *set sail from Belfast for her sea trials.*

Chapter Two

THE VOYAGE BEGINS

Southampton, April 10, 1912

O N THE MORNING OF WEDNES-
day, April 10, 1912, in a
second-class compartment
on the boat train to Southampton, Nellie Becker leaned
toward her napping twelve-
year-old daughter. "Ruth,
you'll probably never be in
England again," she said in a firm voice. "I think
you ought to stay awake and look at this lovely
landscape." The girl stirred and reluctantly turned
to look out the window at the rapidly passing scenery. The London
suburbs had given way to
the lush southern English
countryside — green fields
separated by meandering
roadways and rows of
hedges. To a young girl
born and raised in India,
this scenery did not
capture her interest, but
Ruth dutifully obeyed her
mother's wishes and stayed
awake and watched.

Ruth missed India, but
her mother did not. Nellie
Becker had detested the
heat, the insects, the
lizards, and snakes. More
than once she had suffered
a nervous collapse, the
worst episode occurring
after she witnessed a
native being cremated
outside their home. Only
her love for her husband,
Allen, a Lutheran mis-

sionary heading an orphanage in Guntur, kept
her from leaving such a country.

However, when their doctor warned the
Beckers that their sickly youngest child, twenty-
month-old Richard, would not survive in the
Indian climate, Mrs. Becker took Ruth, Richard,
and four-year-old Marion, together with most
of the family possessions, and sailed from Madras
on the month-long voyage through the Suez
Canal and the Mediterranean to England. She
was unaccustomed to looking after small children
without help, so while she watched the

more active Marion, Ruth
looked after Richard. A
sensible, independent girl,
already almost as tall as
an adult, Ruth could easily
be trusted with such a
responsibility.

Now as the train steamed
through rural England,
Nellie Becker's thoughts
turned to the last leg of the
journey that would carry
them across the ocean to
rejoin friends and family
in Michigan. She deeply
regretted that her husband
could not have come. His
health was also poor, but
the one doctor authorized
to sign his medical release
from his commitment as a
missionary had not been
available when they left.
Otherwise, she sighed, he
would be sitting here with
them now.

Twelve-year-old Ruth Becker (above), her
mother, brother, and younger sister were
among the passengers who boarded the
boat train to Southampton at Waterloo
Station's platform 12 (left).

At 9:30 A.M., while the boat train continued its journey from London, a Daimler landaulet touring car came to a stop at the White Star Line's Southampton dock. Although the Daimler dwarfed most other automobiles of the day, it looked tiny next to the massive black hull of the *Titanic*. The car's passengers were Bruce and Florence Ismay, along with their three youngest children and their governess. But Ismay's family would not accompany him on the *Titanic's* maiden voyage to New York. They had instead chosen to spend the time on a motor holiday through Wales. Only Ismay's secretary and manservant were going with him.

Even as the Daimler was still pulling away, Ismay had turned his attention to White Star's newest ship, his life's greatest accomplishment. At times it seemed he cared more about his ships than his children. Certainly he considered no detail of their upkeep too small to be beneath his attention. It was not uncommon for him to run a finger across the top of a doorframe searching for unwanted dust.

By ten o'clock the first of the paying passengers began to come on board — mainly British residents who had journeyed to Southampton by means other than the boat train, along with travelers whose departure on other ships had been delayed due to the lingering coal strike, which was then ending. But the real rush of passengers came with the arrival of the boat train. People and luggage swarmed the pier while porters dashed about. Many simply stood for a few minutes and looked up in awe at the great ship with its four huge funnels. Parents struggled to keep their children together while first-, second-, and third-class passengers sought out their respective gangways.

When Alice Cleaver arrived in the first-class staterooms of her employers, the Hudson J. C. Allisons of Montreal, she was nervous yet excited. She had never imagined that one day she would be traveling across the ocean in such luxurious surroundings. Mr. Allison had booked two adjoining outside staterooms with a private bathroom. Alice shared one room with Sarah Daniels, Mrs. Allison's maid, and the Allisons' eleven-month-old son, Trevor. The other was occupied by the Allisons and their daughter, Loraine, not quite three. Two other servants, a cook, and chauffeur had been booked in second class.

As nurse to the two Allison children, Alice Cleaver had much to conceal. Already her lack of experience was becoming obvious. Mrs. Allison often had to repeat instructions and assist in caring for the two children. But inexperience was not Alice's most important secret. Three years earlier she had murdered her own baby son. Although tried and convicted, she had been released on the grounds that her crime was an act of desperation following desertion by the child's father, to whom she was not married. The Allisons' trained nurse had quit only a few weeks before sailing, and Alice had been hired in haste. If even a hint of her past slipped out, she would be unemployed and back on the Southampton docks with no hope of making a new life in Canada.

As the noon sailing time approached, the decks became crowded with passengers gathered to observe the *Titanic's* departure. From one of the second-class decks Lawrence Beesley, a science teacher on holiday from London's Dulwich College, watched as a handful of stokers rushed along the dock to the one remaining gangway, their kits slung over their shoulders. But they were too late. Although they argued strenuously, a petty officer stationed at the gangway waved them away. When these stokers had failed to show up, their positions had been filled by men who had waited at dockside hoping to be last-minute replacements on the greatest passenger ship ever built as she embarked on her maiden voyage.

Hudson J.C. Allison (above), a wealthy investment broker from Montreal, was returning from a horse-buying trip to England with his wife Bess, his daughter Loraine, and baby son Trevor (top). The Titanic's *side towers above Southampton's Ocean Dock (right) on the morning of departure.*

The tug Vulcan *pulls the* Titanic *away from White Star's berth 44 (above). Bruce Ismay and his family had spent the night before the sailing in Southampton's Southwestern Hotel, pictured behind the ship (above) and in a 1912 postcard (far left). The hotel, now the office of the Cunard Line, looks much the same viewed from Ocean Dock today (left).*

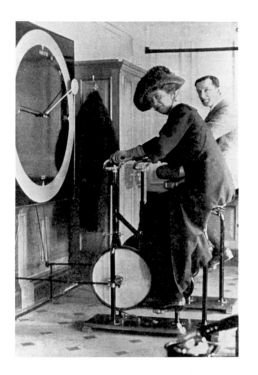

Before sailing, second-class passengers were free to tour first class. Lawrence Beesley (above, in rear) was particularly impressed with the gymnasium, where he hopped onto one of the exercise bicycles. With passengers lining the rails, the Titanic *slowly moves from her berth toward the River Test (below).*

Beesley now watched as the gangway was withdrawn. The hawsers holding the ship to the pier were dropped, and the ship was eased quietly away from her berth. As the huge liner began to glide forward toward the River Test, the crowd on the dock moved as well, keeping pace. The maiden sailing of the *Titanic* may have drawn little attention in the way of whistles or horns from the other vessels nearby, but the citizens of Southampton had turned out in force. One newspaperman would later write, "The vision of the great liner as she moved away from Southampton quay forms an imperishable memory. She looked so colossal and so queenly. Passengers waved farewells from her decks and windows, and a mob of jolly stokers yelled from the fo'castle side. One of these — he must have been a Cockney — played a mouth organ and waved his old cap. He seemed a merry soul."

Lawrence Beesley watched while the crowds on the dock continued moving along with the *Titanic* as she proceeded into the Test, turning to port to head down the narrow channel. Along the section of dock that faced the river the liners *New York* and *Oceanic* were moored side by side among the ships kept from service by the recent coal strike. Their decks were crowded with people wanting to get a good look at the *Titanic* under way. As the *Titanic*'s bow came even with the *New York*'s there remained scarcely eighty feet between the two ships. The massive ropes holding the moored ship strained taut and then suddenly snapped, sounding to Beesley almost like gunshots. They arced high in the air and landed in the crowd, which retreated in alarm. Then, stern first, the *New York* began to swing away from her mooring directly toward the side of the *Titanic*. As the smaller liner moved dangerously close, the *Titanic*'s port propeller gave a sudden surge to create a wash that would prevent the smaller ship from striking her. The *New York* missed by only a few feet before she glided forward, her stern moving along the *Titanic*'s port side and finally swinging out in front of her bow as the *Titanic* came to a stop just in time.

While there was considerable excitement among the crowd on the *New York*, the *Oceanic*, and the wharf, Beesley and the others aboard the *Titanic* calmly viewed the incident from high above. A Seattle motion picture photographer, William H. Harbeck, stood near Beesley cranking

THE *NEW YORK* INCIDENT

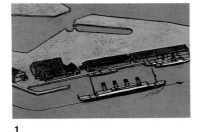

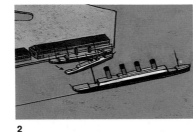

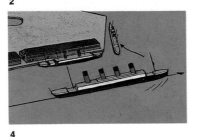

1

2

3

4

The Titanic's *close encounter with the* New York *is depicted at left. Turning into the* River Test *(1), she approaches the* Oceanic *and the* New York *moored at berth 38. The* Titanic's *passing causes the* New York *(2) to swing toward her. The tug* Vulcan *attaches a line to the* New York *(above) and the* Titanic *reverses her engines, thus averting a near collision (right). Captain Smith (top right) is on the bridge but his ship is under the command of the harbor pilot. The* Titanic *moves backward and the* New York's *bow swings out in front of her (3). The* New York *is moved by tugs (4) and, after more than an hour's delay, the* Titanic *departs.*

his camera, catching the events on film. On a first-class section of the boat deck, William T. Sloper of New Britain, Connecticut, heard several people agree that the near-collision was an ominous start for the maiden voyage. By the time the *Titanic* was under way again and proceeding down the river, the ship was buzzing with talk of the *New York* incident, and what it might imply about the maneuverability of this huge new breed of ocean liner.

On the bridge Captain Edward J. Smith heaved a sigh of relief. Only seven months before, once again with a harbor pilot in control of the ship, he had watched as the *Olympic* passed so close to the British cruiser HMS *Hawke* that the small warship had been drawn into the side of the White Star liner, tearing a gash that necessitated repairs at Harland and Wolff. Suddenly it seemed as if that nightmare was to be repeated — the only serious accident in Smith's twenty-five years as a White Star captain. It would have been a humiliating end to his final voyage before retiring.

Smith was the natural choice as the *Titanic*'s commander on her maiden voyage. Known as the Millionaire's Captain, he was a great favorite among the wealthy financiers and prominent members of society who frequently traveled on his ships. As a result he commanded a salary well over twice that of the Cunard captains. With his constant cheerfulness and easy smile, he was equally popular with passengers and crew. This, his last voyage as commodore of the line, would be a fitting cap to a long and distinguished career. But Smith, for all his experience, was

still learning the fine points of seamanship required to navigate this new breed of superliner.

The brief trip to Cherbourg, France, passed without incident, with the exception of a fire that was discovered in a starboard coal bunker in boiler room No. 5. Between eight and ten men were detailed from each watch to keep the burning coal hosed down, and to work at emptying the bunker.

Because of the delay in leaving Southampton caused by the incident with the *New York*, the *Titanic* did not arrive in France until dusk. As twilight turned to darkness, tenders ferried more passengers to the ship, among them a large number of Americans. The most prominent of these were Colonel John Jacob Astor and his young second wife, Madeleine. Astor, the great-

THE *HAWKE* COLLISION

The *Olympic*'s collision with the British cruiser HMS *Hawke* some seven months earlier had sparked fears that such giant liners were simply too big to handle. The two ships had been sailing on parallel courses off the Isle of Wight when the *Hawke* was suddenly sucked into the *Olympic*'s side, puncturing the larger ship above and below the water. One of these gashes is shown above. The *Hawke*'s bow was badly smashed, but amazingly, no one on either ship was seriously injured, and each returned to port for repairs under her own steam.

EN MARSCHALL 1977

grandson of the wealthy fur trader, had built on his inheritance through astute real-estate dealings, including hotels, to become one of the richest men in America. The scandal of his divorce and re-marriage to a woman younger than his son was so great that the newlyweds had fled to Europe and Egypt to allow the publicity to die down. Now, with Madeleine five months pregnant, they were finally returning home.

The next day, Thursday, April 11, the *Titanic* arrived in Queenstown on the south coast of Ireland just as lunch was being served. Twenty-seven-year-old Edwina Troutt chose dining over watch-ing the tenders arrive from shore with more pas-sengers, and bumboats laden with Irish linen, lace, and souvenirs. Winnie Troutt had been assigned to a table for eight near the entrance to the second-class dining saloon, and she was delighted with her com-panions, particularly Jacob Milling, a forty-eight-year-old Copenhagen business-man engaged in locomotive construction. Milling had been in England on business when it had occurred to him how quickly he could journey to America, study some loco-motive factories there, and return. Now, aboard the *Titanic*, he told the former schoolteacher from Bath that

(Left) The White Star tender Nomadic *ferries passengers out to the* Titanic *during her brief call at Cherbourg, France. The next day in Queenstown, tenders (above) pulled away from the White Star jetty bringing the final passengers on board. Edwina Troutt (above) chose to go to luncheon rather than watch the activity.*

QUEENSTOWN

Since there was no dock in Queenstown large enough to accommodate the Titanic, she anchored off Roche's Point (right) while passengers and mail were tendered from shore. As the final bags of mail are loaded aboard the Ireland (far left), passengers, port officials, and journalists crowd the

gangway of the America tied to the side of the Titanic (above left). The last of the passengers board from the tender just before departure (left).
Captain Smith and Purser Herbert W. McElroy (above) pose outside the officers' quarters for a quick picture. While the Titanic lay at anchor, passengers enjoyed fresh sea air (near right), strolled along the second-class boat deck (middle right), or watched the tenders from the stern (far right).

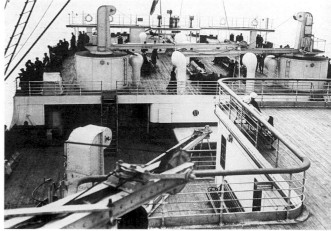

after only one day on board he already felt as if he had known her for years, and he had even written to his wife about her.

That afternoon the ship steamed along the south coast of Ireland. As dusk approached, the coastline rounded away to the northwest and by nightfall the Irish mountains were dim and faint in the distance. Many of the emigrants on board realized that this would be their last sight of Europe, perhaps forever.

Promptly at 7:00 A.M. on Friday morning, Steward Henry Samuel Etches knocked discreetly at the door of a stateroom on A-deck at the top of the aft first-class staircase. He entered and placed a tray laden with fruit and tea on the table, being careful not to disturb the charts rolled up at the side of the bed or the papers spread everywhere.

The occupant of A-36 was Thomas Andrews, the nephew of Lord Pirrie. Andrews was managing director of Harland and Wolff and the head of its design department. He, more than anyone, was responsible for the successful translation of Ismay's and Pirrie's grand schemes into a floating reality — an impressive accomplishment for someone not yet forty. Andrews was a universally popular figure and an extraordinarily hard worker, often arriving at the shipyard by 4:00 A.M. in his paint-smeared bowler hat, the pockets of his jacket stuffed with plans. Now that the second of the three great ships had been built, he had come along for the maiden voyage, as he had on the *Olympic*'s, to monitor her effectiveness and to plan any modifications that might be necessary.

Already Andrews had in mind several changes for the *Titanic* based on his experiences on board the *Olympic*. One of these was to convert one end of the reading and writing room into additional staterooms. The room just wasn't proving as popular as he had expected, and a much smaller room would be sufficient. He also wanted to stain the wicker furniture on one side of the ship green, and lighten some of the coloring on the private promenade decks.

As Andrews finished his breakfast, passengers throughout the *Titanic* were beginning their first full day at sea. Already the relaxed rhythms of shipboard life had taken over. Friendships had been formed and acquaintances renewed. The luxury of the accommodations was a common topic of conversation. Although the accommodations in third class weren't nearly as elegant as in the higher two classes, they were still quite comfortable. The only complaint the steerage passengers might have had was the shortage of bathtubs. There were only two in all of steerage for a total of more than seven hundred passengers, and these were located at the very stern of D-deck — a long hike for those with cabins in the bow.

In second class the Reverend Ernest C. Carter, vicar of the poor parish church of St. Jude's in East London, had developed a slight cold. Fortunately, he and his wife, Lilian, had befriended Marion Wright, a young woman traveling to New York to be married to an Oregon fruit farmer; Miss Wright, it turned out, had some tablets that seemed to relieve the minister's symptoms. A much younger second-class passenger, seven-year-old Eva Hart, had made friends with six-year-old Nina Harper, but only after Eva's father insisted that she share her precious teddy bear with the other girl, whose mother had passed away. Elsewhere in second class Marie Jerwan, a New York housewife returning from a visit to her native Switzerland, discovered that two Frenchmen occupied the cabin next to hers, providing a welcome opportunity to speak the language of her childhood.

The more the passengers explored the brand-new ocean liner, the more their sense of wonder grew. The *Titanic* was not only the largest ship afloat; it was without a doubt the most luxurious.

Mrs. Marie Jerwan, a New York housewife who had been visiting relatives in Switzerland, was among those who boarded at Cherbourg.

Thomas Andrews, managing director of Harland and Wolff, had overseen the construction of the Titanic *from the keel up. He was taking the maiden voyage to make one final inspection of the new ship.*

Benjamin Guggenheim had a reputation as a playboy. Although married, he was traveling on the Titanic *with his mistress, one Madame Aubert of Paris.*

John Jacob Astor, the Titanic's *wealthiest passenger, was the owner of a yacht notorious for its collisions. He had once been sued by the Vanderbilts for having rammed their yacht, the* North Star, *during the America's Cup Races.*

The first-class lounge was decorated in imitation of the palace at Versailles. The smoking room was paneled in rich mahogany inlaid with mother-of-pearl, while stained-glass panels lit from behind surrounded the funnel casing that extended through the room. The Grand Staircase was embellished by balustrades of wrought iron and gilt bronze. The second-class public rooms, decorated in oak and sycamore, were as sumptuous as many first-class hotels. Even the third-class rooms, with their gleaming white walls, were a cut above those on other passenger ships of the day.

The *Titanic*'s reputation for luxury had attracted many notables. Although John Jacob Astor was undoubtedly the richest man on board, he was far from the only millionaire. The first-class passengers, with their retinues of servants and their mounds of luggage, represented the top layer of Anglo-American society. In addition to the Astors were Isidor Straus, the founder of Macy's department store, and his wife; millionaire playboy Benjamin Guggenheim, whose family had made their money in mining and smelting; and George Widener, heir to the largest fortune in Philadelphia, who was traveling with his wife and son. Other prominent Philadelphians included the John B. Thayers, Arthur Ryersons, and William E. Carters. Even the relatively few British passengers were well known, such as William T. Stead, the editor of the *Review of Reviews*; Scotland's Countess of Rothes; and Sir Cosmo Duff Gordon and his wife, Lucile, a successful dress designer for fashionable New York and London society.

The voyage was made even more pleasant by the splendid weather. All day Friday it stayed clear and the huge ship remained perfectly steady as she sailed across calm seas. So it continued through Friday night and into the next morning as the *Titanic* neared the mid-Atlantic.

On Saturday, after another enjoyable lunch-

eon, Elizabeth Lines, whose husband was medical director of the New York Life Insurance Company, stopped for coffee, as was already her custom, in the reception room on D-deck. Soon after she had taken a seat, Captain Smith and Bruce Ismay entered and sat down at a table only a few feet from hers. She recognized Ismay from several years before when they had both lived in New York, and she confirmed his identity with her table steward.

Mrs. Lines paid little attention to the two men until they began discussing the latest day's run, which had been posted shortly after noon. As she listened, Ismay quoted the *Titanic*'s run for each day and compared it to the *Olympic*'s. From noon on April 11 to noon on April 12 the *Titanic* had steamed 484 miles, compared to the *Olympic*'s 458 on the first full day of her maiden voyage. Noon Friday to noon Saturday had seen a run of 519, just a few miles short of the *Olympic*'s 524. The *Titanic* still had over three days in which to increase her speed and cross the ocean in less time than her sister, and Ismay was confident this could be done.

"Well, we made a better run today than we did yesterday," Ismay told Smith. "We will make a better run tomorrow. Things are working smoothly, the machinery is bearing the test, the boilers are working well."

Ismay spoke in a dictatorial fashion while Smith only nodded. Mrs. Lines could easily see Ismay's great satisfaction in the *Titanic*'s performance. He continued on, and she could hear him repeating himself a great deal.

"You see they are standing the pressure," he described of the boilers. "Everything is going well. The boilers are working well. We will make a better run tomorrow."

Finally, bringing his fist down on the arm of the settee, Ismay emphatically announced to Smith, "We will beat the *Olympic* and get in to New York on Tuesday!"

FROM THE ODELL ALBUM

Because of her brief life, photographs actually taken on board the *Titanic* are relatively few in number. The largest contribution of pictures was made by Francis M. Browne, a thirty-two-year-old teacher and candidate for the Jesuit priesthood who sailed on the *Titanic* from Southampton to Queenstown. Fortunately for history, he took his camera with him, and his photographs form an invaluable pictorial record. (For examples, see pages 28, 31, 34 bottom, 39 bottom left, and 72).

Francis Browne was on the *Titanic* as a guest

of Lily Odell, the wife of a well-to-do London fish merchant, who had invited him to accompany her family on the ship to Queenstown. Photographs recently released from the Odell family album make a significant new addition to the archive of *Titanic* images. The picture shown here on the right (above) is one of the few known photographs of first-class passengers on the boat deck. Flanking Lily Odell are her two brothers, Richard and Stanley May (left and right), and her eleven-year-old son, Jack Dudley Odell, stands at the far right. The picture was taken by Kate Odell, Lily's sister-in-law. Before departure, Kate also photographed young Jack on the stairs leading to the raised roof of the first-class lounge (above left), and took a rare view of the liner's third and fourth funnels (right). The Odell party disembarked at Queenstown on April 11. After a week of motor touring in the Irish countryside, the family returned to London and on April 19 attended the *Titanic* memorial service at St. Paul's Cathedral.

Two final views taken from the tender. Having just weighed anchor (left), the Titanic raises steam and (below) heads

into history in this last known photograph ever taken of her.

Other finds in the Odell album include the four photographs shown above which detail the Titanic's near collision with the New York and show the smaller ship being maneuvered to a temporary mooring. From the tender, Kate Odell took a close-up view (left) of the Titanic's towering hull. The two shell doors nearest the camera led to the first-class reception room on D-deck. In a rented Star landaulet (right), the Odells begin their week's motoring trip.

SHIP OF DREAMS

Touring the Titanic

THE FIRST-CLASS LOUNGE

Decorated in a comfortably Edwardian version of Louis Quinze Versailles style, the first-class lounge was where passengers met for cards and conversation over cups of tea. The photograph at left was taken on the Titanic's nearly identical sister ship, the Olympic, and shows the door to the aft first-class staircase.

When the Olympic was scrapped in 1935, her fittings and furnishings were sold and today, windows, paneling, and wall sconces from the lounge (above and above left) can be seen in the White Swan Hotel in Alnwick, England.

The classical statue shown at left is the "Artemis of Versailles" from the Louvre. A small copy of this statue stood on the mantelpiece as shown in the photograph at right.

47

THE *TITANIC* REVEALED

This cutaway view of the *Titanic*'s starboard side presents the layout of the liner's decks, public rooms, staterooms and compartments.

1. Anchor crane
2. Forecastle deck
3. Crow's nest
4. Third-class cabins
5. Forward well deck
6. Morse lamp on bridge wing cab
7. Bridge
8. Wheelhouse
9. Hold containing cargo and Renault automobile
10. First-class baggage
11. Post office
12. Mailroom
13. First-class staterooms

14. Officers' quarters
15. Swimming pool
16. Turkish baths
17. A-deck enclosed promenade (first class)
18. Forward first-class staircase
19. Gymnasium
20. Private promenade for parlor suite
21. Reception room
22. First-class dining saloon
23. Third-class dining saloon
24. Third-class galley
25. First-class lounge

26. Compass platform amidships
27. Boiler rooms
28. Bilge keel
29. A-deck open promenade (first class)
30. First- and second-class galley
31. Reciprocating engine room
32. Turbine engine room
33. Aft first-class staircase
34. Café Parisien
35. First-class smoking room

36. Verandah and Palm Court
37. A la Carte Restaurant
38. Hospital
39. Second-class dining saloon
40. Second-class enclosed promenade
41. Second-class entrance on boat deck
42. Second-class cabins
43. Aft well deck
44. Third-class general room
45. Poop deck
46. Docking bridge

THE FIRST-CLASS STAIRCASE

The crowning feature of the Titanic's interiors was, without doubt, its forward Grand Staircase. Entering it from an afternoon stroll on the boat deck, one would notice how the natural light, streaming through the wrought iron and glass dome overhead (right), reflected off the polished oak of the wall paneling and the gilt of the elaborate balustrades (below right and far right). On the uppermost landing (left and right), a large carved panel contained a clock surrounded by two classical

figures symbolizing Honor and Glory crowning Time. When dressed for dinner (left), passengers could walk down to the dining saloon on D-deck, or take the elevators (above) located just forward of the staircase.

52

On each landing of the staircase, spacious entrance halls (top right) were lit by gold-plated light fixtures (above) and had cozy seating areas. On D-deck (bottom left) the staircase led into the white-paneled reception room (bottom right) which adjoined the dining saloon.

Survivors recall admiring the oil paintings that decorated the landings of the Titanic's staircases. Similar paintings from the Olympic (above), purchased when she was scrapped in 1935, today adorn the walls of the Crown Berger paint works in Haltwhistle, England.

THE DINING SALOON

The spacious expanse of the first-class dining saloon is conveyed by this color illustration (right) from a period Olympic brochure. The only known photograph ever taken of the Titanic's dining saloon (below) is this authentic but unclear image, purportedly taken during lunch on April 11.

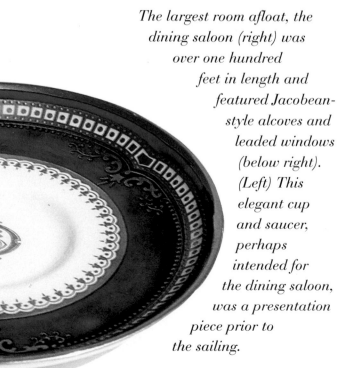

The largest room afloat, the dining saloon (right) was over one hundred feet in length and featured Jacobean-style alcoves and leaded windows (below right). (Left) This elegant cup and saucer, perhaps intended for the dining saloon, was a presentation piece prior to the sailing.

One of the livelier tables was that shared by Clarence Moore (top), a Washington sportsman and social figure; Francis Millet (center), a well-known painter of historical scenes and an accomplished raconteur; and Archibald Butt (bottom), President Taft's military aide.

The dining saloon's menu card was printed within a folder which pictured Europa and Columbia linked above a radiant white star.

Before dinner, passengers gathered in the reception room (left) and then entered the dining saloon through the double doors shown at left.

FIRST-CLASS STATEROOMS

The lavish period decor typical of the Olympic's and the Titanic's B-deck suites is depicted below. A nightstand drawer (right), retrieved from the disaster site, matches the one in the first-class stateroom (far right).

"OLYMPIC." FIRST CLASS SUITE STATEROOM.

The four parlor suites provided the most expensive accommodation on board. Each suite had its own sitting room, two bedrooms, two wardrobe rooms, and a private bath and lavatory. An Empire-style parlor-suite bedroom (left) opened onto a sitting room such as the one shown in the color illustration (right) and photograph (left).

On the Titanic, Bruce Ismay occupied one of the two parlor suites that also boasted a private fifty-foot promenade.

Although the Titanic's bathroom facilities were advanced for 1912, some first-class staterooms shared a washroom (above).

Suite B-58/60 was occupied by the Baxter family of Montreal. Mrs. Baxter, a wealthy widow (right, at left), shared one of the bedrooms pictured above with her daughter, Helene (right), the wife of a prominent Montreal physician. Her unmarried son, Quig, took the other. The location of their suite is marked on the deck plan (far right).

THE VERANDAH CAFE

Also known as the Verandah and Palm Court, this room was actually two rooms as there was one on each side of the ship, just aft of the first-class smoking room. Ivy grew up the trellis-covered walls (above), and white wicker furniture (right) and high arched windows (left) completed the airy, outdoor effect. First-class passenger Mrs. Frederic O. Spedden recalled her six-year-old son and Loraine Allison using the Verandah Café as a playroom.

THE READING AND WRITING ROOM

Since the smoking room was a male preserve, this elegant Georgian-style room (right), adjacent to the lounge, was designed as a retreat for the ladies. When touring the ship before sailing, second-class passenger Winnie Troutt tried to persuade her sister, Emmeline Collins, to take some of the White Star stationery from this first-class public room. The older woman refused, so the letter (above) that Winnie wrote describing the wonders of the Titanic to Emmeline's daughter was sent on unpilfered stationery.

THE CAFE PARISIEN

Designed to emulate a Parisian sidewalk café, this room (right), next to the restaurant on B-deck, was unique to the Titanic. With its genuine French waiters and casual decor, the café was a popular spot with Colonel Gracie and his set, which included the successful author, Helen Churchill Candee (above).

THE TURKISH BATHS

Decorated with richly colored tiles, gilded beams, and bronze lamps, the cooling room of the Titanic's Turkish baths (left) was a Moorish fantasy. Its exotic atmosphere is conveyed by a view of a similar room on the Olympic (right) and in the color illustration below.

WHITE STAR LINE.
No. 659

R.M.S. "TITANIC."

This ticket entitles bearer to use of Turkish or Electric Bath on one occasion.

Paid 4/- or 1 Dollar.

On April 13, 1912, first-class passenger Mrs. Frederic O. Spedden (right) wrote in her diary, "I took a Turkish bath this morning. It was my first and will be my last, I hope, for I never disliked anything in my life so before, though I enjoyed the final plunge in the pool."

THE SWIMMING POOL

The pool or "swimming bath" on F-deck was a novel feature of the first-class accommodations on the Olympic and the Titanic.

The pool and Turkish baths are highlighted in this 1912 advertisement which claims that by providing Vinolia soap on board, the Titanic offers " a higher standard of toilet luxury and comfort at sea."

THE BARBER SHOP

For gentlemen accustomed to a daily hot lather and shave, the Titanic provided two barber shops, one in first class and another in second. This barber shop (left) on the Olympic closely approximates the room

Titanic passengers would have known. It was also the place one visited to buy novelties and souvenirs of the voyage such as postcards, pennants, paperweights (above), and commemorative plates (left).

THE GYMNASIUM

The Shipbuilder, *a British trade journal, noted that in the gymnasium (right) "...passengers can indulge in the action of horse-riding, cycling, boat-rowing, etc. and obtain beneficial exercise, besides endless amusement." Situated on the starboard side near the first-class entrance (above right), the gymnasium had high arched windows that looked out onto the boat deck. On the night of the disaster, this room provided a warm refuge while lifeboats were being loaded on the deck outside. The gym's instructor encouraged passengers to try out equipment such as the mechanical camel (above, far right), even while the ship was sinking.*

63

SECOND-CLASS PUBLIC ROOMS

Passengers traveling second class on the Titanic *and the* Olympic *enjoyed accommodations that were the equivalent of first class on other liners of the day. The second-class lounge or library, as it was known, (left and right) while not as palatial as the first-class lounge, was a large, handsome room, paneled in sycamore and furnished with comfortably upholstered mahogany chairs.*

Like its rather grander counterpart in first class, the smoking room in second class (right) was considered a "man's room" and was furnished accordingly. Carved oak paneling and oak furniture covered in dark green morocco leather created an appropriate clubroom atmosphere.

Food served in the oak-paneled dining saloon (above and middle left) was from the same galley that prepared first-class meals. Passengers sat at long tables in fixed, swivel chairs — a seating style found even in first class on most liners in 1912. The dinner plate (right) is typical of the service used in the second-class dining saloon on the Titanic.

LIFE IN THIRD CLASS

Although severe in comparison to the sumptuous rooms on the higher decks, the accommodations in third class were superior to what many of the passengers would have known at home. Third-class cabins were mostly located in the lower or less desirable parts of the ship, and single men and women were separated by an entire ship's length — men in the bow and women in the stern. Families, however, stayed together in small but reasonably comfortable rooms such as the one at right.

Flanking the third-class staircase (top) were doors to the smoking room (above) and to the third-class general room (opposite, bottom right).

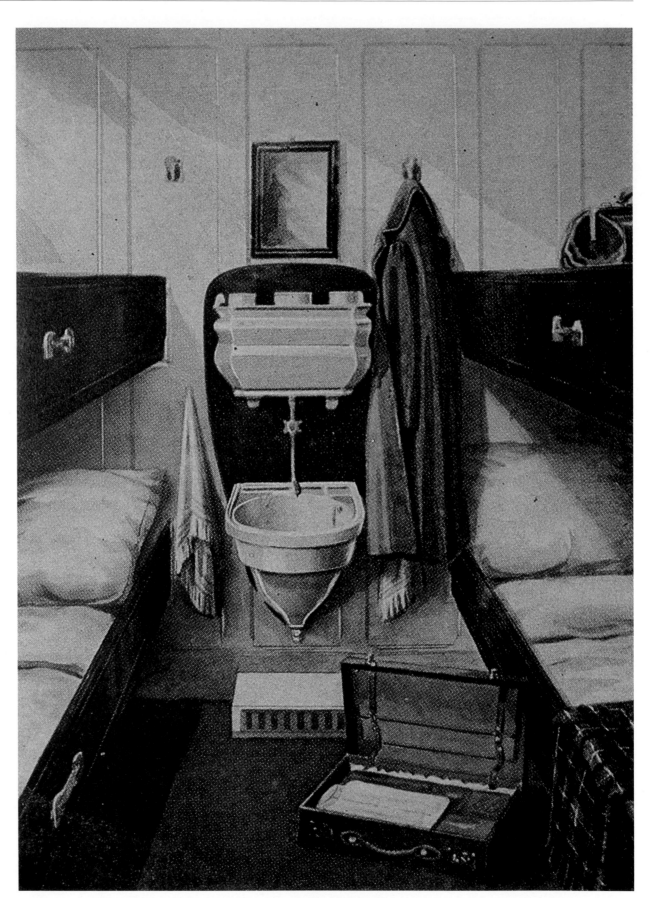

Located amidships on F-deck, the third-class dining saloon (above and far left) was actually two rooms divided by a watertight bulkhead. Its walls were enameled white and decorated with posters of White Star's parent company, the International Mercantile Marine.
(Left) The general room, with its pine paneling and sturdy teak furniture, was the third-class equivalent of a lounge.

Chapter Three

THAT FATEFUL
SUNDAY

Sunday, April 14, 1912

O N SUNDAY MORNING COLONEL Archibald Gracie rose early. He had an appointment with Fred Wright, the ship's racquetball professional, and he was determined not to miss it. Normally Gracie, who was a military historian and the cousin of former American president Theodore Roosevelt, prided himself on his dedication to physical fitness, but until today he had spent more time reading selections from the ship's library than in the gymnasium. "I enjoyed myself as if I were in a summer palace on the seashore, surrounded by every comfort," he would later write. Today he intended to make up for his indolence.

Following his half-hour session with Wright, Gracie took a swim in the heated pool, after which he made another racquetball appointment and also made dates with the pool attendant and the gymnasium instructor. The colonel then proceeded to the dining saloon for breakfast which was followed by a Church of England service presided over by Captain Smith. A similar service was conducted in the second-class dining saloon by the assistant purser, Reginald Barker. Little Eva Hart was delighted that one of her favorite hymns, "Oh God Our Help in Ages Past," was sung, and she joined in enthusiastically. At the same time, Father Thomas Byles was conducting a Catholic Mass in the second-class lounge, followed by one for steerage.

While most of the passengers and crew were eating Sunday luncheon, the *Titanic*'s two wireless operators, Harold Bride and Jack Phillips, were in the wireless room busily trying to catch up with the backlog of passenger messages. The

Employed by the Marconi Company, twenty-five-year-old Jack Phillips (above left) and his assistant Harold Bride, twenty-one, (above right) operated the ship's powerful wireless. (Left) Now nearing Newfoundland, the Titanic *increases her speed to over twenty-two knots in an attempt to better the* Olympic's *maiden voyage pace.*

previous evening the wireless set had broken down and it hadn't been fixed until nearly 5:00 A.M. Sunday morning. At 1:40 P.M., as the men worked feverishly to catch up, they were interrupted by an incoming message from the White Star steamer *Baltic*: "Captain Smith, *Titanic*. Have had moderate variable winds and clear fine weather since leaving. Greek steamer *Athinai* reports passing icebergs and large quantity of field ice today in latitude 41.51 north, longitude 49.52 west. Last night we spoke [with] German oil tanker *Deutschland*, Stettin to Philadelphia, not under control; short of coal; latitude 40.42 north, longitude 55.11. Wishes to be reported to New York and other steamers. Wish you and *Titanic* all success."

The *Baltic*'s message was immediately given to Captain Smith, who, rather than turn it over to the officers on watch, carried it with him as he headed for A-deck. Smith had shown an earlier message, from the *Caronia*, to Second Officer Charles Lightoller shortly before 1:00 P.M., and it had been posted in the chartroom.

As Smith walked aft along the promenade, he encountered Bruce Ismay, who was conversing with George and Eleanor Widener. According to Ismay's later testimony, Smith handed him the message without comment. Ismay merely glanced at it, put it in his pocket, and a moment later went below.

Selena Cook, a young newlywed who had left her husband in England while she traveled to

In the only known photograph of the Titanic's *wireless room (above), Junior Operator Harold Bride sits at the key. One of the messages received that Sunday was an ice warning from the steamer* Baltic, *a transcription of which survives (below).*

Arthur Ryerson and his wife Emily (above) had learned by telegram in Paris of their son's accidental death in Pennsylvania. When they were able to book passage home on the Titanic, *Mr. Ryerson immediately made funeral arrangements for April 19, two days after the ship was to arrive.*

New York to visit relatives, spent Sunday afternoon writing letters home. She was terribly homesick, and when mailing them she remarked to one of her roommates, Amelia Lemore, "I wish I was going back where they are going." Due to the cold, many of the second-class passengers, particularly those with children, sought the enclosed promenade deck. Among these was Ruth Becker, performing her daily routine of pushing her brother, Richard, in a wheeled stroller provided by the White Star Line. Having already been at sea for a month before boarding the *Titanic*, Ruth was not particularly impressed with the voyage so far. She did, however, appreciate how wonderfully new the ship was. She took delight in sleeping between brand-new sheets and eating from dishes that had never before been used.

Many of the third-class passengers also stayed indoors. Soon after lunch, a number began dancing in their general room and in the enclosed area below the forward well deck. Even a few off-duty crewmen joined the fun, although they did not drink, as this was forbidden. In the third-class smoking room a number of card games were soon in progress.

That morning two more boilers had been lit, and now rumors were circulating that the engines had never run so fast. Catherine Crosby, whose husband owned a Great Lakes shipping company, had been told by a seaman that the temperature of the ocean had dropped, and that this indicated the ship was near icebergs.

THE OTHER RYERSON

Unknown to the wealthy Ryersons in their deluxe suites on B-deck, a distant cousin was also on the *Titanic* — a dining saloon steward named William Edwy Ryerson. A Canadian of Loyalist stock, William had served in the British army in India, and worked for the Cunard Line before joining the *Titanic*. Although he survived the sinking, it is not known whether he knew of his relatives on board.

Around five o'clock Marian Thayer, whose husband was a vice-president of the Pennsylvania Railroad, went to the stateroom of her friend and fellow Philadelphian, Emily Ryerson, and asked if she would care to join her for a walk. Mrs. Thayer was pleased when her friend accepted. This was the first time since the beginning of the voyage that Mrs. Ryerson had made an appearance on deck except when the other passengers were dining, for she was in mourning. Her older son had been killed in an automobile accident near Bryn Mawr only one week before. She was returning home with her husband Arthur, their younger son John, and two of their daughters. The two ladies strolled for nearly an hour, finally resting on a couple of deck chairs outside the aft staircase on A-deck where they could enjoy the sunset.

As the sky was turning pink, Bruce Ismay approached the two women. He was dressed in a dark blue serge suit, and in spite of the cold maintained his usual custom of wearing neither a hat nor an overcoat. Without invitation he stopped and sat down on the end of a deck chair beside them.

"I hope you are comfortable and all right," Ismay said to Mrs. Ryerson. Made aware of her family's circumstances, he had already arranged for their party to have an additional stateroom and steward assigned to them when they had boarded at Cherbourg. Although grateful for this kindness, Mrs. Ryerson was not in the mood to make conversation. Instead she hoped he would leave.

"We are in among the icebergs," Ismay announced cavalierly, fishing the *Baltic*'s telegram out of his pocket and holding it out for Mrs. Ryerson to see. She glanced at it, noticing the mention of the tanker *Deutschland*. "We are not going very fast, twenty or twenty-one knots," he continued, "but we are going to start up some new boilers this evening."

"What is the rest of the telegram?" Mrs. Ryerson asked.

"It is the *Deutschland* wanting a tow, not under control," he replied.

"What are you going to do about that?"

Ismay replied that they were not going to do anything about the *Deutschland*, but would instead reach New York early and surprise everyone. He wanted to show just what the *Titanic* could do.

When the women's husbands approached, Ismay departed, leaving Mrs. Ryerson with the impression that the *Titanic* had no time to delay in aiding other steamers such as the *Deutschland*. And when she and her husband reached their stateroom, they began discussing what they would do if they reached New York late Tuesday night instead of Wednesday morning.

Bruce Ismay would later testify that at 7:10 P.M., as he sat in the smoking room, Captain Smith approached and asked, "By the way, sir, have you got that telegram which I gave you this afternoon?"

"Yes," Ismay replied, producing it from his pocket. "Here it is."

"I want to put it up in the officers' chart-room," Smith explained, and left with the message.

IN ORDER TO AVOID THE ICE FOUND EACH SPRING near the Grand Banks, the great underwater plateau off the coast of Newfoundland, ships took a more southerly route than at other times of year, normally steaming southwest until reaching forty-two degrees north latitude and forty-seven degrees west longitude — a location known as "the corner." From there they steamed nearly due west on the course for Nantucket Lightship. Although the *Titanic* reached the corner around 5:00 P.M. Sunday, Captain Smith had ordered a delay in changing the course until 5:45, causing the ship to travel an additional sixteen miles southwest. Third Officer Herbert Pitman, a veteran of seventeen years at sea, calculated that when the *Titanic* turned the corner, the ship was ten miles south of the normal shipping route.

Smith's decision was likely due to the ice warnings the ship had been receiving. As early as Friday, April 12, the French liner *La Touraine* had reported ice, and on Saturday a passing steamer, the *Rappahannock*, morsed by signal lamp that she had passed through heavy field ice. The *Titanic* had since passed the area of ice reported by both ships without spotting any bergs, but the messages from the *Caronia* and *Baltic* indicated that ice would continue to be a threat during the voyage.

As the weather grew noticeably colder, passengers walking on deck before dinner enjoyed a memorable sunset.

At 6:00 P.M. Second Officer Lightoller also came on duty. His four-hour watch would last until 10:00 P.M. Remembering the *Caronia* message Captain Smith had shown him earlier in the day, he asked Sixth Officer James Moody to calculate when they would reach the ice. Moody reported that it would be around eleven o'clock that evening.

Lightoller had been with the White Star Line since January 1900, and he had left the 17,000-ton *Oceanic* to join the 46,000-ton *Titanic*. His original position had been that of first officer, the position he had held on the smaller liner, but Captain Smith had later decided to bring aboard Henry T. Wilde as chief officer, which bumped William Murdoch down to first and Lightoller to second. It was to be only a temporary demotion, but a disappointing one nonetheless.

Before joining White Star, Lightoller had led an adventurous life. He had been shipwrecked on a deserted island, prospected for gold in the Yukon and worked as a cowboy in the Canadian West. Now he was a career man who expected to command his own ship some day. He could be intolerant of those who did not follow orders to the letter or whom he considered to use poor judgment.

After supper Sunday evening, a number of passengers braved the cold on deck to marvel at the glorious sunset. Rev. John Harper, a Baptist minister from Scotland who was traveling with his daughter and his sister-in-law, Jessie Leitch, watched as it faded to just a bit of red in the west. As they turned to go below for their evening prayers and Bible reading, Rev. Harper remarked to Miss Leitch, "It will be beautiful in the morning."

Just after sunset the blinds in the wheelhouse aft of the bridge were closed. Now the only light in the room came from the compass light and a

Three of the Titanic's *senior officers (left to right): Chief Officer Henry Wilde, Second Officer Charles Herbert Lightoller, and Sixth Officer James Moody. An officer's gilt coat button (below) with the White Star insignia.*

On the Olympic *and the* Titanic, *the second-class dining saloon was unusually spacious for the period, extending the entire width of the ship.*

The piano was used to great advantage at the hymn-sing on Sunday evening at which Marion Wright (below) was a soloist.

small light on the courseboard. At 7:15 P.M. Lamp Trimmer Samuel Hemming arrived on the bridge to report that all the ship's navigational lights had been lit. He found that Lightoller had gone to the officers' messroom for dinner and that First Officer William Murdoch was temporarily acting as officer of the watch. His report made, Hemming was just leaving when Murdoch called him back.

"Hemming, when you go forward see the fore scuttle hatch closed as we are in the vicinity of ice, and there is a glow coming from that," Murdoch ordered. "I want everything dark before the bridge." Any light would interfere with their ability to see an obstacle in their path. Hemming went out on the bow and personally closed the hatch before going below.

In the wireless room Junior Operator Harold Bride was busy writing up the day's accounts, and although he had his earphones on, the transmitter had been shut down. The alternator tended to run hot, so he was giving it and the motor a much-needed rest. Consequently he did not receive another ice warning sent to the *Titanic* that day, this one from the steamer *Californian*. But at 7:30, with the motor started once more, Bride intercepted the same ice warning as it was being sent to the *Antillian*: "6:30 P.M., apparent time, ship; latitude 42.3 north, longitude 49.9 west. Three large bergs five miles to southward of us." Bride acknowledged the warning and delivered it to the bridge.

At 7:35, when Second Officer Lightoller returned to the bridge after dinner, he noticed how quickly the temperature was falling now that the sun had gone down. Murdoch mentioned that the temperature had dropped four degrees in the half hour Lightoller had been gone — down to thirty-nine degrees Fahrenheit. An hour later it was nearly freezing, and Lightoller ordered Quartermaster Robert Hichens to take his compliments to the ship's carpenter and caution him

not to let the ship's fresh water supply freeze. The weather remained clear and unusually calm as the *Titanic* raced onward through the deepening darkness.

In the crowded à la carte restaurant on B-deck, Captain Smith lingered over dinner with several of the ship's more prominent passengers. The party had been organized by George and Eleanor Widener. Their guests were their son, Harry, the Thayers, the William E. Carters, and Major Archibald Butt, President Taft's aide-de-camp. The gathering was a quiet, pleasant one. As dictated by White Star Line regulations, Captain Smith did not drink wine or liquor of any kind. Shortly before nine o'clock he excused himself for the evening and left for the bridge.

In third class an informal party followed dinner, with music provided by fellow passengers. At one point a rat scurried through the room, causing the girls to squeal and several young men to give chase. Out on deck a few people braved the cold, pausing at the docking bridge on the poop deck to ask Quartermaster George Rowe questions regarding the ship's speed and when they could expect to dock in New York. Several couples sought quiet spots for romantic interludes.

Nearly one hundred passengers gathered in the second-class dining saloon for a hymn-sing led by Rev. Carter, whose cold was now much better. Douglas Norman, a young Scottish engineer who sat opposite Lawrence Beesley at the purser's table, provided accompaniment on the piano. Rev. Carter preceded each hymn by giving details about the author and often a history of how it came to be written. When Marion Wright sang a solo of "Lead Kindly Light," he explained that it had been written as a result of a vessel wrecked on the Atlantic.

In fact, Lawrence Beesley noted that many of the hymns dealt with dangers at sea, and that "Eternal Father, Strong to Save," commonly known as "For Those in Peril on the Sea," was

THE A LA CARTE RESTAURANT

Elegant was the word for the first-class à la carte restaurant aboard the Olympic and the Titanic (right) as shown in this 1911 advertisement for Colman's Mustard. The artist has exaggerated the scale somewhat to make the room seem larger than it was, as can be seen from the photograph (top opposite). The fork (below) comes from White Star's first-class silver service.

Among the guests at the dinner party hosted by Mr. and Mrs. George Widener (top) in the restaurant on Sunday evening were Captain Smith (above center), Mrs. Thayer (above left), and her husband John (above right).

The original fittings and paneling from the Olympic's à la carte restaurant were removed and auctioned when the ship was scrapped in 1935 and can be found today in a private home in England. Shown here are (clockwise from middle left) examples of the finely figured French walnut paneling with its carved and gilded details, a reeded pillar, and a section of wall paneling graced by one of the restaurant's entry doors. (Left) A White Star water carafe.

sung in unusually hushed tones. Rev. Carter explained that it had been chosen by special request.

Kate Buss, a young Englishwoman en route to California to be married, noticed how emotionally everyone was singing the hymns, and that even some of the men had tears in their eyes, including a gentleman who had left his wife and children behind to make a new start for his family in Canada. At one point she and other passengers saw Lilian Carter with her face buried in her hands. They could not decide if she were doing so in prayer or in deep emotion.

In the crow's nest Lookouts Archie Jewell and George Symons stared into the blackness.

"It is very cold here," Jewell remarked.

"Yes," Symons said. "By the smell of it there is ice about." When Jewell asked why he thought so, Symons replied, "As a rule you can smell the ice before you get to it."

Before them stretched a starry, moonless sky. Had there been a moon, it would have been possible to see ice by the reflection of moonlight on its surface. But icebergs did not necessarily appear white in the darkness, and detection at night could be difficult. A berg could also be spotted by the ring of white foam at its base where the waves broke against it. But on this night the sea before them was perfectly calm. To worsen matters, the lookout station was without binoculars, which for some reason had been removed before the ship left Southampton.

At 8:55 P.M. Captain Smith arrived on the bridge, remarking to Second Officer Lightoller about the cold.

"Yes, it is very cold, sir," Lightoller agreed. "In fact it is only one degree above freezing. I have sent word down to the carpenter and rung up the engine room and told them that it will be freezing during the night."

"There is not much wind," Smith added.

"No, it is a flat calm as a matter of fact,"

79

Lightoller replied.

"A flat calm," repeated Smith.

"Yes, quite flat. There is no wind."

In his twenty-four years as a mariner, Lightoller had never seen so calm a sea. He remarked to the captain that it was a pity there was no breeze while they were going through the ice region. They continued to discuss the weather, agreeing on how clear the night was. Eventually they began to discuss what time they would be reaching the ice, and how they would be likely to detect it. In view of the many stars, Lightoller predicted there would be a great deal of reflected light from any icebergs. Smith indicated that if the weather became the slightest bit hazy, they would have to slow down. Upon leaving the bridge at 9:20, he left Lightoller with the instruction, "If in the slightest degree doubtful, let me know."

The *Titanic*'s captain had vacated the bridge knowing that navigationally this was the most crucial period of the voyage. In fact, he knew it better than anyone. A number of ice messages had been received that Sunday — most notably from the *Caronia*, *Baltic*, *Amerika*, and the *Californian* — although only the *Caronia*'s was posted in the chartroom, according to later testimony. The officers were therefore ignorant of the others.

At 9:30 Lightoller instructed Sixth Officer Moody to telephone the crow's nest and tell the men to keep a sharp lookout for small ice and growlers, and to pass the word along to the subsequent watches. Moody spoke to Lookout George Symons, communicating the warning of small ice but neglecting to mention growlers — low-lying bergs. Noting this, Lightoller ordered Moody to call again, to add the warning of growlers.

In the wireless room Senior Operator Jack Phillips had his hands full. The ship had just come within range of Cape Race, Newfoundland,

which meant he had established direct communication with the North American continent. Now he was busy transmitting passenger messages to friends, relatives, and business contacts. Harold Bride had gone to bed early, intending to relieve Phillips at midnight rather than 2:00 A.M. because of the long hours the senior operator had spent repairing the transformer that morning.

Shortly after 9:30 Phillips was interrupted by a message from the steamer *Mesaba*, addressed to the *Titanic* and all eastbound ships, which read, "Ice report. In latitude 42 north to 41.25 north, longitude 49 west to longitude 50.3 west. Saw much heavy pack ice and great number large icebergs, also field ice. Weather good, clear."

Phillips had had a very long day and more work lay ahead. He had already delivered a number of ice messages to the bridge, and this new one seemed unimportant. He simply replied, "Received, thanks." The *Mesaba*'s operator, Stanley Adams, knowing that messages pertaining to navigation took precedence over passenger traffic, waited to hear that Phillips had reported the message to the captain. When no such reply was forthcoming, Adams sent "Stand by," indicating he was waiting for an answer. Phillips had resumed his transmissions to Cape Race, however, never leaving the key. The message, the most important sent to the *Titanic* so far, went undelivered. Unlike the previous ice messages, which had simply reported random icebergs, the *Mesaba* had identified a huge rectangular ice field into which the *Titanic* was directly steaming.

At ten o'clock the lights in the public rooms in third class were put out, encouraging the passengers to retire for the night. A few minutes later in second class, following such hymns as "On the Resurrection Morning," Marion Wright's second solo of "There Is a Green Hill Far Away," and the final hymn of "Now the Day Is Ended," Rev. Carter noticed some stewards waiting to

THE *TITANIC*'S BRIDGE

(Right) A cutaway painting of the Titanic*'s bridge as it appeared just after the change of watch at 10:00 P.M. on April 14.*
1) *Quartermaster Robert Hichens at the ship's wheel.*
2) *Quartermaster Alfred Olliver assisting.*
3) *Sixth Officer James Moody.*
4) *Fourth Officer Joseph Boxhall.*
5) *First Officer William Murdoch in command.*
(Below) The Titanic*'s wheel was attached to a bronze pedestal known as a telemotor. The instrument was linked hydraulically with the steering mechanism in the stern, above the rudder. The* Titanic *also had a simple auxiliary wheel forward of the wheelhouse on the "captain's bridge," which was linked mechanically to the telemotor.*

serve coffee and refreshments. He closed the evening hymn-sing by thanking the purser for the use of the saloon. Then he remarked on the confidence everyone felt on board due to the liner's size and steadiness, and how they all looked forward to their arrival in New York. "It is the first time that there have been hymns sung on this boat on a Sunday evening," he told the crowd, "but we trust and pray it won't be the last."

In first class, as concerts being held in the two reception rooms ended, the passengers drifted to their rooms, or to the lounges and smoking room. Elmer and Juliet Taylor, an American couple living in London, went through the routine good-nights with several friends and went to their cabin, where they prepared for bed. When he put his ear to the pillow, Taylor could hear that the engines were running faster than ever before. He dozed off while his wife sat reading and warming her feet by the room's heater.

While most of the *Titanic's* passengers drifted toward their cabins or braved the cold on deck for a final stroll before retiring, the first-class smoking room remained crowded. A number of card games were in progress. At one table several professional gamblers were playing with Walter Miller Clark of Los Angeles and Howard B. Case, the London manager of Vacuum Oil. At another table Alfred Nourney of Cologne was playing with William B. Greenfield, a New York furrier, and Henry Blank, a jeweler from New Jersey. Nourney, a twenty-year-old who had booked passage as "Baron Von Drachstedt," had come up from second class to mingle among the wealthy in first.

Elsewhere in the room others had gathered to converse over drinks. George Rheims of Paris and his American brother-in-law, Joseph Loring, were trying to figure the speed of the ship and determine the next day's run when an elderly steward approached and suggested they might plan on a higher figure. The two men asked why.

"Because we are making faster speed than we were yesterday," the steward explained.

"What do you know about it?" Loring asked suspiciously.

"I got it from the engine room," he replied.

"That doesn't mean anything."

"Gentlemen, come out and see for yourself," the steward suggested. "You notice that the vibration of the boat is much greater tonight than it has ever been." He led them into the passageway just outside the smoking room. "Now you will notice the vibration."

Loring, whose stateroom was just below where they stood, was convinced. "I have never noticed this vibration before," he explained. "We are evidently making very good speed." Rheims, who had spent every evening in the smoking room, had never felt such vibration before, either.

In the crow's nest Lookouts Frederick Fleet and Reginald Lee had replaced Symons and Jewell at ten o'clock. Symons told the others of the orders they had received, careful to note that these had come from the bridge.

Before turning over the watch to First Officer Murdoch, Lightoller had reported that they were steering a course of north seventy-one degrees west.

"It is pretty cold," Murdoch remarked. He was wearing an overcoat for protection against the cold air.

"Yes, it is freezing," Lightoller replied. The temperature of the air was thirty-one degrees Fahrenheit. While Murdoch's eyes grew accustomed to the darkness, the two spoke of the calm, clear weather and how far they could see. The stars could be seen setting on the horizon.

"We will be up around the ice somewhere about eleven o'clock, I suppose," Lightoller remarked matter-of-factly. He described Smith's earlier visit to the bridge and the captain's desire to be notified if there was any doubt about the situation. He also told Murdoch of his orders to the crow's nest. When he had finished his report,

When the collision occurred, most of the Titanic's *passengers had retired for the night, but the first-class smoking room was still busy with groups of men enjoying cigars and playing cards (top). As the period rendering and the photographs*

show, the smoking room had the cozy opulence of an exclusive men's club. The paneling was rich mahogany in the Georgian style and was inlaid with mother-of-pearl. Delicately hand-painted and stained glass windows were used throughout. Silver-plated ashtrays, like the one at left, graced the tables which had raised edges to prevent glasses from sliding off in rough seas.

Lightoller went around the decks for a quick inspection, marking the end of his watch, and then went to bed.

In the wireless room Jack Phillips was still working Cape Race when a message burst into his headset at what must have seemed full volume. It came from the nearby Leyland liner *Californian*. "Say, old man, we are stopped and surrounded by ice." The overworked Phillips angrily replied, "Shut up! Shut up! I am busy. I am working Cape Race."

The *Californian*'s operator, Cyril Evans, listened as Phillips sent "Sorry. Please repeat.

Jammed," to Cape Race. The *Californian*'s receiver was not strong enough to hear the station at Newfoundland, only the *Titanic*. Twenty-five minutes later he could still hear Phillips morsing, and at 11:35 Evans shut down his set and turned in.

By 11:00 P.M. the *Titanic*'s public rooms had nearly all emptied, and most of the passengers and off-duty crew members were in bed. Dickinson and Helen Bishop, a young honeymooning couple from Dowagiac, Michigan, had noticed how uncomfortably cold the lounge had become, and they left for their B-deck stateroom. The lounge was normally closed at eleven, but

William Sloper, the young Connecticut banker, and several companions had become so absorbed in a game of bridge that they were oblivious to the time and temperature. Toward 11:30 the lounge steward approached and politely asked them to finish so he could put out the lights and close the room.

Only the smoking rooms in first and second class remained open. In the latter a solitary card game was in progress. In first class the crowd had dwindled throughout the evening. Alfred Nourney's card game with Henry Blank and William Greenfield continued, as did the game that included Walter Clark, Howard Case, and several of the gamblers. Major Butt and Clarence Moore of Washington had joined Philadelphians Harry Widener and William Carter in a card game. Lucien Smith, another Pennsylvanian, had teamed up with three Frenchmen for bridge.

Elsewhere in the ship all was quiet. In second-class cabin F-33, Selena Cook and her roommates had finally drifted off to sleep, having been kept awake by the Hudson Allisons' chauffeur, George Swane, and his cabin mates who were enjoying a loud pillow fight next door. Lawrence Beesley lay reading in his bunk, his mattress vibrating more than usual due to the ship's increased speed. For no particular reason, when preparing for bed that evening he had taken his lifebelt down from the top of the wardrobe in his room.

In her stateroom at the forward end of B-deck, Margaret "Molly" Brown, the wife of a Colorado millionaire, had stayed up to read. In cabin C-125 Elizabeth Shutes, governess to teenager Margaret Graham, noticed a smell that reminded her of the ice cave in the Eiger Glacier. The room was so cold that she turned on the heater, but although it soon warmed the cabin, she could not sleep. She was inexplicably nervous, and lay awake expectantly.

On the poop deck at the stern, Quartermaster

George Rowe was pacing back and forth to keep warm and pass the time. The third-class passengers had all long since gone. In the first-class dining saloon Steward James Johnson and several other crew members sat around one of the tables talking and gossiping about their passengers. In the messroom just below the forecastle the seamen on watch had congregated. Normally they would be scrubbing the decks, but they were excused from duty on Sunday nights. A number were playing cards, but shortly after 11:30 Seaman William Lucas quit the game. He had run out of money.

On the open bridge First Officer Murdoch stood alone and stared into the clear, cold night. Fourth Officer Joseph Boxhall had stepped aft to the officers' quarters, and Sixth Officer Moody was in the wheelhouse inside the bridge, standing by Quartermaster Hichens at the wheel. Also in the wheelhouse was Quartermaster Alfred Olliver, who was adjusting the light on the standard compass. None of the men spoke, and the entire bridge was in darkness to allow the men to see out the windows. The *Titanic* was now steaming in excess of 22 1/2 knots — so fast that were Bruce Ismay to change his mind about arriving in New York a day early, she would have to slow to 20 knots for the remainder of the voyage.

In the wireless room Jack Phillips had just finished his Cape Race transmissions. The *Mesaba*'s warning continued to remain undelivered to the bridge.

In the crow's nest Lookouts Fleet and Lee stared into the darkness. It had been a quiet watch so far. They had seen nothing. But around 11:30 the horizon directly ahead seemed to develop a slight haze. Fleet casually remarked to Lee about this, although he had decided it was hardly worth mentioning.

A few minutes later Fleet could begin to make out a black object immediately in their path. It could be only one thing.

Frederick Fleet (above) first sighted the iceberg from his position in the crow's nest (below). Questions persist about the missing binoculars that might have helped him spot the berg sooner. In command on the bridge was First Officer William Murdoch (below).

By the time Sixth Officer Moody shouted "Iceberg right ahead!" Murdoch himself had seen the threatening shape loom out of the darkness. He dashed for the telegraph that communicated with the engine room and gave his order to put the engines "full speed astern."

"There is ice ahead," he said, reaching past Lee for the crow's nest bell. He quickly rang it three times, indicating something directly ahead, and then picked up the telephone. As soon as he heard the sound of the telephone being picked up in the wheelhouse, he spoke.

"Is someone there?"

"Yes," Moody replied. "What do you see?"

"Iceberg right ahead."

"Thank you," Moody said automatically and hung up. "Iceberg right ahead!" he called loudly to Murdoch. By now the first officer had seen the berg and rushed to the engine room telegraph. While signaling "full speed astern," he ordered "hard a' starboard" to Hichens, who promptly spun the wheel hard over.

"Hard a' starboard. The helm is hard over, sir," Moody called from where he stood behind Hichens. (The order stemmed from the early days of sailing when putting the helm to starboard caused the ship to turn to port.)

In the crow's nest Frederick Fleet was still holding the telephone, anxiously waiting for the bow to begin to swing to port. As the dark mass loomed closer, only a fringe of white appearing at the top, the two lookouts braced themselves. Finally the nose of the ship began to turn. At first it looked as if the *Titanic* were going to clear, but as the iceberg moved alongside the starboard bow, there came a strange scraping noise.

Chapter Four

A DEADLY ENCOUNTER

Sunday, April 14, 11:40 P.M.

Ice tumbles into the well deck as the iceberg scrapes along the Titanic's *starboard side. The time between the sighting of the iceberg by the lookout and the collision was less than a minute.*

N O ONE WILL EVER KNOW WHAT thoughts flashed through First Officer Murdoch's mind as the wall of ice passed along the starboard side of the bow, pieces of it falling onto the forecastle and well deck. As the officer of the watch, the navigation of the *Titanic* was his responsibility. Now he had steered the ship into an iceberg. It was any seaman's worst nightmare.

Once the bow began to swing, Murdoch ordered "hard a' port," intending to bring the stern away from the berg, but it was too late. Betraying no emotion, he now rang the watertight-door alarm and then threw the switch that closed the doors. Murdoch ordered Quartermaster Olliver to note the time and told Sixth Officer Moody to enter it in the log.

The collision had occurred at 11:40 P.M.

Ironically, by reversing the engines, Murdoch had actually made the collision more certain. Like all ships, the *Titanic* turned more quickly the greater her forward motion. Murdoch had not only stopped the engines but had reversed them. Each second that the propellers reduced the ship's headway was a precious one. Had the *Titanic* turned just a little more, perhaps only inches, she might have missed the iceberg completely.

A moment later Captain Smith rushed onto the bridge.

"What have we struck?" he asked.

"An iceberg, sir," Murdoch replied. "I put her hard a' starboard and run [sic] the engines full astern, but it was too close. She hit it. I intended to port around it, but she hit before I could do any more."

"Close the watertight doors," Smith ordered.

"The watertight doors are closed, sir."

Smith then asked Murdoch if he had rung the warning bell, and the first officer replied that he had.

Captain Smith now faced the horrible fact that his ship had been damaged, how seriously he did not yet know. Furthermore, he had not

The massive watertight doors between the boiler and engine rooms were closed by a switch on the bridge moments after the ship collided with the iceberg. This system of sealing the watertight compartments in the event of an accident was thought to make the ship "practically unsinkable."

been present on the bridge during the most critical part of the voyage.

Far below the bridge, in the heat of the forwardmost boiler room, No. 6, Leading Stoker Frederick Barrett was talking with Second Engineer James Hesketh when a red warning light and the "Stop" indicator came on. "Shut

all dampers," Barrett called out. Suddenly a rush of water began pouring in from along the side of the ship, two feet above the floor and only a short distance from where the two men stood. Barrett was nearly swept off his feet before he and Hesketh jumped through the quickly closing watertight door leading aft to boiler room No. 5. There they saw a gash extending from a point two feet aft of the forward bulkhead into the coal bunker that had been emptied because of the earlier fire. A geyser of water shot through the opening. When Barrett climbed to a higher deck where he could see down into No. 6, he found it

already eight feet deep in sea water.

Apart from the men on the bridge and those close to the point of the iceberg's impact, few crew members realized that anything was amiss. Lookout George Symons, lying in his bunk, thought the anchor had dropped and the grinding noise he was hearing was the anchor chain running out of the ship. Fireman Harry Senior, also in the bow, dreamt he was aboard a derailing train. Fourth Officer Boxhall, on watch at the time, couldn't understand what the scraping noise was as he approached the bridge on the starboard side of the boat deck. The ice did not extend up

The firemen and engineers who worked in the boiler rooms deep inside the ship were the frontline troops in the Titanic's *losing battle against the sea. Although no pictures of the* Titanic's *boiler rooms are known to exist, some sense of the conditions can be gained from the photograph (above) which shows members of the "black gang" shoveling coal in a ship of the period.*

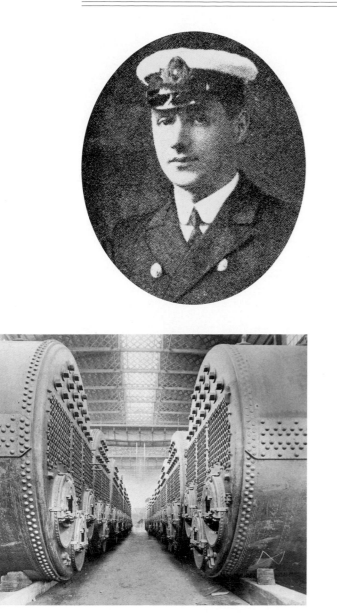

The twenty-four huge, double-ended boilers each weighed nearly one hundred tons and are seen lined up in Harland and Wolff's boiler shop prior to installation (above). Second Engineer James Hesketh (top) was on duty in boiler room No. 6 when water suddenly burst through the side of the ship.

high enough for him to see it pass by.

The iceberg deposited fragments of ice in a number of open portholes along the upper decks. Henry Sleeper Harper, of the American publishing family, sat up in bed and saw the berg quickly passing his window, pieces crumbling as it went. Other passengers who happened to look out couldn't understand what this dark mass was that was swiftly moving past. In the first-class smoking room nearly everyone stood up from their seats when the jarring motion disturbed the room, and a number headed for the promenade deck to see what had happened.

"Oh, don't those boys make a noise," Selena Cook said upon awakening, assuming that the pillow fight next door was still in progress. But the grating noise continued, sounding to her like gravel. Second-class passenger Kate Buss, just opening a newspaper to read in her bunk, thought the noise sounded like a skate on ice. Few of those who heard the sound made by the collision recognized it as anything serious.

"Hallo! There goes a blade," cried one of the men working in the bakehouse just aft of the galley. The *Titanic*'s shudder reminded him of the motion a ship made when it dropped a propeller. He and the other bakers took no further notice and went on preparing bread for the following day.

On the poop deck at the very stern, Quartermaster George Rowe felt the jarring motion, and before long what appeared to be a windjammer with sails the color of wet canvas was silently passing the aft well deck. Recognizing it as ice, Rowe at first thought it was going to strike the docking bridge that extended out over the side of the ship, but when he realized it wasn't scraping the hull, he walked to the rail to watch it pass.

An unfamiliar quiet fell throughout most of the *Titanic*. The steady rhythm of the engines, the sound of wind blowing through the rigging,

and the wake trailing behind the ship were all dying away. Almost immediately a number of off-duty crewmen began appearing on the forward well deck, hoping to see what the ship had struck. Leading Fireman Charles Hendrickson had been awakened not by the collision, but by one of his mates, Thomas Ford, who insisted that he come on deck. The two men trooped up with a crowd of others in time to see the iceberg disappearing astern. By the time Fireman Alfred Shiers arrived on the scene, the ship was making just a slight headway. Only the dim outline of the berg could still be seen well to the stern, as if it were shrouded in a mist. Those who stood at the starboard rail had to wade through a pile of broken ice several inches deep.

On the bridge a worried Captain Smith ordered Fourth Officer Boxhall to inspect for damage. The young officer worked his way down into the bow, going as low as he could in the passenger areas and finding no sign of damage. He returned to the bridge and reported this to Captain Smith, who had since telegraphed "half speed ahead" to the engine room.

"Go down and find the carpenter and get him to sound the ship," Smith ordered.

Boxhall had just begun to descend the staircase leading down to A-deck when he met Carpenter John Hutchinson.

"The captain wants you to sound the ship," Boxhall told him.

"The ship is making water," Hutchinson replied breathlessly. He continued on to the bridge while Boxhall headed below. There he met Jago Smith, one of the mail clerks, who wanted to know where the captain was. "The mail hold is filling rapidly!" Smith told Boxhall excitedly.

"Well, you go and report it to the captain, and I will go down and see," Boxhall replied. He returned to the sorting room on G-deck where the other mail clerks were feverishly pulling mail from racks. In the room below, the water had risen to within two feet of the top of the stairs, and bags of mail floated on the surface. Boxhall returned to the bridge and reported the grim news to Captain Smith. Without saying a word, Smith turned and walked away.

There was soon other evidence that the ship was rapidly taking on water. At the very bow Boatswain's Mate Albert Haines and Lamp Trimmer Samuel Hemming heard air escaping. They discovered the forepeak tank was filling with water. At this point Chief Officer Henry Wilde, the ship's second-in-command, came along.

"What is that, Hemming?" Wilde asked.

"The air is escaping from the forepeak tank," Hemming replied. "She is making water in the forepeak tank, but the storeroom is quite dry."

Wilde immediately headed for the bridge to report this to the captain.

In his suite on B-deck, Bruce Ismay had also been awakened by the scraping noise. His first thought was that the ship must have dropped a propeller blade. Dressed only in pajamas, he stepped into the passageway where he met a steward. When the crewman could not offer an explanation for what had occurred, Ismay donned an overcoat and headed for the bridge. There he asked Captain Smith what had happened.

"We have struck ice," Smith explained.

"Do you think the ship is seriously damaged?" Ismay asked.

"I am afraid she is."

No further conversation between the two men has survived, but it is likely Ismay pressed the

Chief Engineer Joseph Bell, aged fifty-one, was at the peak of his career after having worked for the White Star Line since 1885.

captain for further details. Inwardly, however, Ismay must have been reeling. His greatest dream since assuming control of the White Star Line from his father was rapidly turning into a nightmare.

On his way back to his cabin, Bruce Ismay met Chief Engineer Joseph Bell at the top of the stairs. Not wanting to believe Smith's grim assessment, he asked Bell if he thought the ship was seriously damaged. Bell replied that she was, but, undoubtedly not wishing to unduly alarm the managing director of the White Star Line, added that he was satisfied the pumps would keep her afloat. Ismay then headed back to his stateroom to pull a suit on over his pajamas.

A few minutes after Ismay left the bridge, Thomas Andrews arrived. It was he who explained to Smith the full seriousness of the *Titanic*'s situation. Based on the damage reports received so far it was clear that the iceberg had ruptured the first six watertight compartments, the first five of which were cargo or storage areas. The sixth was boiler room No. 6. Over two hundred feet of the ship had been opened to the sea. With the first five of her sixteen watertight compartments hopelessly flooding, the *Titanic* was doomed.

It must have been a grim conversation. Andrews knew the ship better than anyone and was fully aware of the shortage of lifeboats. He estimated that the liner had a little more than an hour to live. Smith now faced the worst. His ship was sinking and the more than 2,200 people on board were in extreme peril.

Although the captain and the officers on the

THE PERILS OF ICE

North Atlantic icebergs are formed when warmer weather causes Greenland glaciers to "calve" chunks of ice into the sea. Huge bergs, such as the one that fatally damaged the *Titanic*, float south with the currents along with smaller bergs called "growlers" and floating sea ice, known as drift ice. Under certain conditions, bergs, growlers, and drift ice come together to form an ice pack. Just such an ice pack lay directly in the path of the *Titanic*.

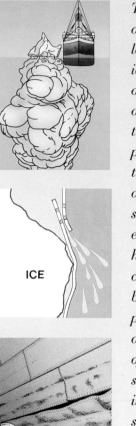

The diagram (left) demonstrates that the largest part of an iceberg is underwater— only about one-ninth is actually visible above the surface. Contrary to popular misconception, the iceberg did not tear a gash in the Titanic's shell plating. As it exerted pressure on the hull (middle left), it caused the plates to buckle and the rivets to pop (bottom left), allowing great volumes of water to flow into the ship. (Right) This illustration from 1912 shows the ice field toward which the Titanic was steaming.

   In April, 1912, the ice was unusually far south for that time of year. Thus even Captain Smith's precautionary measure of "turning the corner" later than was customary proved an inadequate precaution. Despite the dangers, however, it was common to steam full speed through regions where ice was likely, trusting the crew's ability to see a berg in time. After the *Titanic* disaster, no ice message would ever again go undelivered to a ship's bridge. And with the formation of the International Ice Patrol in 1914, ships would now have ample warning of ice conditions ahead.

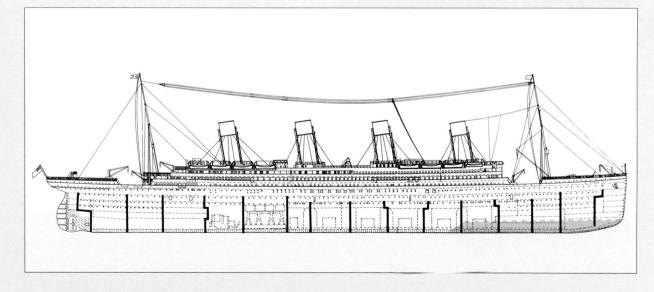

(Above left) Was this the iceberg that sank the Titanic? *Photographed on the morning of April 15 in the area of the sinking, it had a telltale smudge of red paint along its base.*
(Above) A profile of the Titanic, *showing the compartments damaged by the iceberg.*

bridge now knew it was only a matter of time before the *Titanic* sank, the passengers and the remainder of the crew had for the most part been fooled by the slightness of the impact. It was only the sudden absence of engine noise or vibration, so familiar at sea, that alerted them to possible trouble, but even then there was no general alarm. Many crewmen were not informed of the seriousness of the damage; both they and the passengers were left to speculate as to what was happening. This apparent negligence on Smith's part was possibly deliberate. It is probable from his actions after the collision that by limiting the flow of information, he hoped to prevent a panic. Nonetheless, in the first half hour following the *Titanic*'s encounter with the iceberg, many passengers and crew realized that something was very wrong indeed.

THE AWARENESS CAME DIFFERENTLY TO different people. Almost everyone in the forward steerage cabins had been jolted awake, and soon a stream of third-class passengers was heading toward the stern. Paul Maugé, secretary to the chef of the à la carte restaurant, found the alleyway near his cabin so crowded with passengers heading aft with their luggage that he could scarcely get through as he made his way toward the bow to investigate. Steward Samuel Rule, a thirty-five-year veteran of the White Star Line, was surprised upon entering the E-deck companionway at how orderly everyone seemed to be. It was as if they were landing in New York, not stopped in mid-ocean.

In her third-class cabin toward the stern of the ship, Minnie Coutts, who was taking her two sons from London to join her husband in New York, had felt only a slight shock. She lay awake in bed for a quarter of an hour before she heard other passengers opening their doors and asking questions. Stewards assured them that there was

no danger and that the ship would go on soon. Finally Mrs. Coutts stepped into the hallway and was surprised to see other third-class passengers heading for the open deck at the stern: Men, women and children, many carrying all their belongings. The crowd soon passed, and the hallways were quiet once again. Mrs. Coutts returned to her cabin and waited. She was anxious to learn what had happened, but didn't want to leave her two boys, who continued to sleep peacefully in their bunks.

The *Titanic*'s second- and first-class passengers whose staterooms were higher up or farther aft than steerage were not as quick to show alarm as those in third class. After the engines stopped, second-class passenger Winnie Troutt, the youngest of the three ladies in her E-deck cabin, volunteered to investigate. She threw on a dressing gown and went out into the hallway where she met several other passengers, including one of her table companions, a teenager named Edgar Andrew. They asked a crewman why the ship had stopped and he responded that it was only an iceberg. Back in her cabin, Miss Troutt reported this to her roommates and then told them she was going on deck for "further particulars."

Also in the second-class section of E-deck, Kate Buss had put aside her newspaper but remained in bed listening to the engines running in reverse. When they stopped, she put on her dressing gown and slippers and went out into the hallway where she bumped into her table companion, Dr. Ernest Morawick. He offered to investigate and as she stood waiting for him to return, a group of the musicians came by carrying their instruments. Something was obviously happening, so Kate went to the cabin of Marion Wright, whom she met during the voyage, awakened her, and together they went on deck. There were few people about, and nothing seemed amiss. There they met Douglas Norman, who

Second-class passenger Kate Buss from Sittingbourne, England, was one of those who had retired for the night but was still awake when the collision occurred. The period illustration (below) along with the photograph (right) of a second-class stateroom on board the Olympic *show how pleasant second-class accommodations were by 1912 standards.*

had accompanied Marion at the hymn-sing a few hours earlier. In his soft Scottish brogue, Norman informed the two ladies that there was talk that the ship had struck an iceberg.

Together the three young people walked to the rail where several others were looking out over the stern. In the darkness all was still, the sky above brilliant with stars. Then a number of people carrying their belongings began to appear on the well deck. When one of the second-class men started to make fun of how protective they were of their things, Kate Buss turned on him. Didn't he realize that what they carried might be all they owned in the world, she asked indignantly. Douglas Norman eased the situation by tactfully suggesting the three of them go below for warmer clothing.

In her first-class cabin on B-deck, Emily Ryerson had been unable to sleep due to the cold. As she lay awake, her thoughts likely turned again to the loss of her son. When the engines suddenly stopped, she rang for her steward and asked what was the matter.

"There is talk of an iceberg, ma'am," Walter Bishop replied, "and they have stopped not to run into it."

Mrs. Ryerson instructed Bishop to keep her informed of any orders. She put on an extra wrap, then opened one of the large square ports in her room to look out. The stars were shining, the sea calm, and all was quiet.

Down one deck in cabin C-126, Elmer Taylor told his wife, Juliet, "I think I will go on deck, nose about, and see if I can be of any assistance." He leisurely put on the suit he had laid out for the next day, picked up his cigar and climbed the aft first-class staircase to the promenade deck. It was nearly deserted. Spying a steward, he asked why the ship had stopped.

"Struck an iceberg," the steward replied.

Unwilling to take the news seriously, Taylor continued his stroll.

Hudson Allison was roused from his sleep by a knock at the door that connected his stateroom to his servants' room next door. When he opened it he was confronted by a worried Sarah Daniels, Mrs. Allison's maid. Sarah was worried because the ship had stopped.

"Oh, Sarah, you are nervous," he told her. "Go back to bed." Then he added that the ship couldn't sink. Unconvinced, Sarah decided to dress.

Almost imperceptibly the *Titanic*'s bow was settling deeper into the water as her forward compartments flooded. A group of first-class passengers was walking forward along the promenade deck when one of them, William Sloper, asked his companions if they didn't feel as if they were walking downhill. They all agreed.

When Winnie Troutt reached the stern of the boat deck she found only a lovely starlit night and a very calm ocean. She had just been ordered off the deck by a crewman when she spied a group of others gathered around two of the lifeboats. They were peeling the canvas cover off one, while the other was being lowered until it was level with the deck. Suddenly her confidence in the ship's unsinkability disappeared. She immediately left the boat deck to inform her friends.

If Captain Smith had held out any hope that the *Titanic* might be saved, within half an hour after the collision that hope was dashed for good. He had been below and inspected the flooding along with Chief Officer Wilde, Fourth Officer Boxhall, and Thomas Andrews. Carpenter Hutchinson had taken a draft of the water, and there was no question that the *Titanic* was continuing to sink. It was now up to Smith and his officers to organize the orderly evacuation of the ship and save as many people as possible. Their job would be difficult, not only because there were too few lifeboats, but because the *Titanic* had not put the passengers through a lifeboat drill. Soon after midnight Smith gave the order to prepare the boats, but still no general alarm was raised.

By this time Joseph Boxhall had gone to fetch the other officers. He stuck his head into Charles Lightoller's room and found him sitting quietly on his bunk smoking his pipe. Never one to act rashly, Lightoller had reasoned that if he were needed it was best to remain where the other officers expected to find him.

"You know we have struck an iceberg," Boxhall announced.

"I know we have struck something," Lightoller replied.

"The water is up to F-deck in the mailroom," Boxhall explained. Lightoller needed no further information. He pulled a sweater and overcoat over his pajamas and headed for the boat deck.

Word of the order to prepare the boats was soon passing through the crew areas. In the bakehouse Charles Burgess had removed some bread from an oven and replaced it with butter to be melted to make the cornbread so loved by the American passengers. Just then someone came in and shouted, "All hands on deck! Bring your lifebelts!" Burgess and the other bakers abandoned the room and were on their way to the deck when he suddenly remembered the butter. Fearing it might catch alight, he returned, set the pan on a cold stove, and left again.

Firemen William Nutbean and John Podesta couldn't get their shipmates to stir from their bunks. The men were taking the news of the iceberg as a joke. Then Fireman Eustace Blann appeared holding a lump of ice. "Look what I found on deck!" he cried, his face pale and lips quivering. A moment later Boatswain Alfred Nichols came to the door shouting, "Get your lifebelts and man your boats!"

Crowds from third class were still making their way aft. Steward John Hart found that the door connecting the E-deck alleyway to one of the second-class staircases leading to the boat deck and the lifeboats had been opened, yet the third-class passengers were moving right past it

(Above) This ship's post office of the period provides an idea of the industrious scene in the Titanic's *mailroom when water suddenly began to pour into its lower level. Although clerks rushed to drag the sacks of registered mail up to the sorting level, the flooding water soon chased them from the mailroom. One of the clerks, Jago Smith, hurried to the bridge to report, "The mail hold is filling rapidly!"*

SMOKING ROOM

B DECK ELEVATOR

In the second-class areas of the ship farther aft, there was less obvious cause for alarm. Those who took the situation seriously had easy access to the upper decks by way of their two stairways (above and below), one of which (above) led up to the boat deck.

on their way to the aft well deck. Hundreds of passengers soon gathered there, as well as on the poop deck.

Daniel Buckley, a young Irish immigrant, was among the crowd of third-class passengers working their way toward the stern. But when he noticed that everyone was wearing lifejackets, he attempted to return to his cabin in the bow for his own. This meant pushing past people coming up the stairs. The girls were crying while the young men were assuring them that nothing serious had happened. At the last flight of stairs before reaching his cabin, Buckley stopped. Water already covered the bottom three steps and was rising quickly.

Before Winnie Troutt could reach her stateroom she saw a crewman in uniform shouting,

"All passengers put your lifebelts on and go up on top deck. Leave everything. It is only a precaution and you can all return to your staterooms." A number of passengers were joking about the orders when she bumped into her table companions Jacob Milling and young Edgar Andrew.

"What is the trouble, Miss Troutt?" Milling asked. "What does it all mean?"

"A very sad parting for all of us," the young woman replied with emotion. "This ship is going to sink."

"Impossible!" laughed Andrew. Milling could see how upset she was, and he took hold of her hands.

"Don't worry," he explained. "I am sorry such a thing has happened, but I sent the wireless today. We are in communication with several vessels and we will all be saved, though parted. But," he added, "I won't go back home on so big a ship."

Winnie Troutt and Edgar Andrew left Milling talking with several other men. When Winnie finally reached her own stateroom, she quickly replaced her dressing gown with a warmer coat. One roommate was gone, but the other, Nora Keane from Ireland, was so nervous that she needed help in dressing. When Nora insisted on taking the time to put on her corset, Winnie grabbed it from her and flung it down the narrow passage leading to their porthole. There just wasn't time for such things.

All thoughts of homesickness had vanished from Selena Cook's mind. One roommate, Amelia Lemore, had just returned from the deck to announce that she for one was going to get dressed. Selena immediately began putting on warm clothing. Another roommate, Elizabeth Nye, followed suit. Only Mildred Brown, the Hudson Allisons' cook, remained in her bunk, even when George Swane, the Allisons' chauffeur, knocked on the door and warned, "I advise you girls to get dressed as soon as you can." While Selena dressed, taking time to put on much of her jewelry and to pin broaches to her underclothing, she pleaded with Mildred to get up. In complete exasperation, Selena told her that she was surely the only one aboard the *Titanic* still in bed. At this, the reluctant cook finally arose and began dressing, too.

Leaving ahead of the others, Selena and Amelia met a steward who ordered them back to bed. Instead Selena turned to her friend and said, "Let's go up and have a look around now that we are dressed." Their experience was shared by many other passengers on the *Titanic* during the confusing second half hour after the collision. Although many members of the crew had received the order to prepare the lifeboats, many others

had not. A clear breakdown in the lines of shipboard communication had taken place, a breakdown that would not improve as the bow continued to sink and the slope of the ship become more alarming.

Many of the second-class stewards who had received Smith's orders dutifully banged on doors

It was a first-class stateroom door such as those pictured below that R. Norris Williams broke down when the occupant could not open it.

until their passengers were awake, shouting at them to put on lifebelts and come up to the boat deck. In the more genteel first-class areas there was little banging on doors. However, as R. Norris Williams of Geneva, Switzerland, and his father were leaving their C-deck stateroom, they found a steward attempting to open the door of another room, behind which a panicking passenger was trapped. When Williams put his shoulder to the door and broke it in, the steward, who had been opposed to the young man's use of force, announced, "I will be forced to report you for having damaged the property of the company."

Others also found it hard to believe that there

Williams (left) was a well-known tennis player in Europe who planned on playing in America over the summer before entering Harvard in the fall.

was any cause for urgency. On his way back to his stateroom from his walk on deck, Elmer Taylor passed a crewman who told him, "Go to your cabin, put on your lifebelt and proceed to the boat deck." The ship appeared so secure it seemed stupid to do so, but when he reached his cabin he had his wife dress and put on a warm

fur coat. When it came time to put on the belts, she asked, "Are you going to put one on?"

"No," Taylor replied. "I will take one with me, though." He fully expected to be back in his room within half an hour.

Elsewhere in first class, Lambert Williams, Elmer Taylor's business partner, had just finished explaining to the Countess of Rothes and her cousin Gladys Cherry that the watertight compartments would surely keep the ship afloat, when a crewman approached. "Will you all get lifebelts on," he urged. "Dress warmly and come up to A-deck." But when the two ladies returned to their cabin and asked their steward where their lifebelts were, he assured them the jackets were unnecessary.

One of the few people attempting to dispel the confusion was Thomas Andrews, though he was not even a formal member of the crew. He circulated throughout first class seeing to it that the crew got their passengers out. When he told Stewardess May Sloan that as a precaution she should get her passengers to put on warm clothing and assemble on the boat deck, she thought he looked heartbroken. She asked if it wasn't serious, and he replied that it was very much so, but to

Once it became clear that the ship really was in trouble, many people crowded the pursers' offices, like the one above, to request their money and valuables. Purser McElroy (above) told his staff to refuse the requests and urge the passengers instead to get their lifejackets and go up to the boat deck. This Titanic lifejacket (above) was worn by Madeleine Astor.

keep the bad news to herself for fear of panic.

While walking on C-deck, Andrews ran into his own steward, Henry Etches. Now he told Etches to make sure the passengers opened their doors, to tell them their lifebelts were on top of the wardrobes, and to assist them in any way he could. As the two men approached the purser's office they saw Purser Herbert McElroy standing in the midst of a large group of ladies who were demanding their jewelry. In response, McElroy kept asking the ladies to go to their staterooms and put on their lifebelts.

"That is exactly what *I* have been trying to get them to do," Andrews remarked to Etches.

Colonel John Jacob Astor and his pregnant wife, Madeleine, were standing with six others in the A-deck foyer when Captain Smith came down the stairs. Astor strode over to him and the two spoke in an undertone. Smith's demeanor was perfectly calm, but when Astor returned to his wife he told her and the others in the group that they had better put on lifebelts. One of these was Helen Bishop, whose honeymoon was definitely not finishing up as planned. She had just sent her husband below for her muff, and now she went to tell him the disquieting news. As the Bishops were about to leave their cabin, Mrs. Bishop's dog, Frou Frou, tugged at her dress, tearing the hem. Realizing that if lives really were at stake it would not be wise to try to save her pet, she left the animal in her cabin.

On either side of the main first-class staircase, stewards bearing lifejackets were lined up as the procession of passengers worked their way to the deck. But as people arrived on the boat deck, they were driven back inside by the cold and by the unearthly roar from the pipes running up the three forward funnels. The excess steam from the boilers was being released, causing a noise so loud that anyone on deck was forced to shout to be understood.

An hour earlier the last passengers had

vacated the first-class lounge because of the cold. Now it provided a relatively comfortable alternative to the frigid boat deck. The ship's band had begun to play lively music. People in all stages of dress and undress mingled there, women often clinging to their husbands. One woman had bare feet. Many female passengers wore only stockings, including one who was still wearing her evening gown.

The hardy few who remained on the boat deck had sought shelter in the gymnasium. Most gathered in clusters to compare notes, while several circulated between the different groups to learn what others had heard.

"Lifeboats!" one woman cried out. "What do they need of lifeboats? This ship could smash a hundred icebergs and not feel it. Ridiculous!"

Others were equally calm about being ordered on deck. Steward William Ward, adjusting lifebelts for passengers, found that many were treating the situation with a great deal of levity. Just inside by the staircase, an officer tied lifebelts on Elizabeth Lines and her daughter, saying, "We are sending you out as a matter of precaution. We hope you will be back for breakfast."

At approximately 12:10 A.M. Captain Smith stepped into the wireless room for the second time since the collision. The first time he had informed Harold Bride and Jack Phillips that the *Titanic* had struck an iceberg and that he was having an inspection made to determine the extent of the damage. He had told the two to prepare to send out a distress call. Now the grim-faced captain told Bride, "Send the call for assistance," handing him the *Titanic*'s estimated position.

Phillips, who had just stepped into their adjoining sleeping quarters, came back into the wireless room and asked, "What call should I send?"

"The regulation international call for help. Just that," Smith replied, and then disappeared.

Phillips immediately sat down at the key and

THE DOGS ON THE *TITANIC*

"**Q**ueer lot of people on the ship. There are a number of obnoxious, ostentatious American women, the scourge of any place they infest and worse on shipboard than anywhere," artist Francis Millet wrote in a letter to a friend, which was posted at Queenstown. "Many of them carry tiny dogs and lead husbands around like pet lambs."

So prevalent were the pet owners on the *Titanic* that an informal dog show was being planned for Monday, April 15. The canines ranged from Harry Anderson's Chow dog, valued at fifty dollars, to Robert W. Daniel's champion French bulldog, Gamon de Pycombe, priced at an astronomical seven hundred and fifty. The John Jacob Astors (right), the *Titanic*'s most prominent passengers, had with them their Airedale named Kitty.

Even the *Titanic*'s clean, new kennels were not adequate for some passengers, and Helen Bishop's tiny pet, Frou Frou, slept with her in her cabin.

Each day a member of the crew would take the dogs on walks around the fantail of the ship. From her vantage point in second class, seven-year-old Eva Hart could watch the parade, and she grew particularly fond of Robert Daniel's French bulldog. Her newfound and expensive love for that breed has remained with her to this day.

Of all the dogs on the ship, the only two to survive escaped on early lifeboats carrying so few people that no one objected. Miss Margaret Hays of New York brought her Pomeranian with her in lifeboat No. 7, while Henry Sleeper Harper of the publishing family boarded boat No. 3 with his Pekinese, Sun Yat Sen.

As the ship plunged under, R. Norris Williams, struggling in the freezing water, found himself staring disbelievingly into the face of bulldog Gamon de Pycombe. Williams was convinced he had imagined the sight until he met a fellow passenger on the *Carpathia* who explained that he had gone to the kennels after the lifeboats had all gone and released the dogs, sparing them from being trapped in cages as the ship went down.

Dancer Irene Castle recalled in her memoirs a crossing from France to New York in May of 1912. "We set sail soon after the sinking of the *Titanic* and a couple of days out we ran into a fearful fog. I can remember with what terror I sat night after night holding Zowie, my very lovable and very ugly English bulldog, in a deck chair on the top deck. In case we hit an iceberg, I was afraid they would refuse to let me take her with me in the lifeboat, so I wrapped her in a steamer blanket. In the confusion of abandoning ship, they would think I was carrying a baby. A very ugly baby."

Including the Astors, who had been married six months, there were eight honeymoon couples traveling first class. These included John and Nelle Snyder of Minneapolis (top), and Daniel and Mary Marvin of New York (right). The Marvins' wedding had been recorded by movie camera, a novel idea but easily done, since Daniel's father had founded the Biograph Film Studio. After Daniel was lost, this story proved irresistible to London's Daily Mirror (above).

tapped out the distress signal "CQD" followed by the *Titanic*'s call letters, "MGY," repeating the action a half-dozen times. While he did so, he and Bride calmly made joking remarks about the situation.

While Phillips and Bride continued to send the first distress signals from the stricken liner, on the forward boat deck First Officer Murdoch was overseeing the preparation of the starboard lifeboats, ordering that they be swung out over the side of the ship and lowered until they were even with the deck and in position for loading. Third Officer Pitman, who was assisting Murdoch, was surprised at how easily boat No. 7 moved — a great improvement over the lifeboats on ships fitted with older davits. In two minutes the boat was flush with the boat deck, hanging several feet away from the side of the ship due to a slight list to starboard.

"Ladies, this way," Murdoch called to the small crowd of passengers. There was no response. No one wanted to leave the apparent safety of the solid *Titanic* for a tiny, frail boat on the North Atlantic. Nearby, Vera Dick, a young newlywed from Calgary, peered over the side of the ship. It was a long way down to the water, which looked very black and cold.

John and Nelle Snyder, a Minneapolis couple returning from their European honeymoon, decided against leaving. They had just turned to walk aft when someone, recognizing that a large number of those present were young couples, called out, "Put in the brides and grooms first." The Snyders and the Dickinson Bishops edged forward. First Helen Bishop was helped over the gap and into the boat, then Nelle Snyder, who was frightened at how far the water below

appeared. Their husbands followed, and a handful of others climbed in after them. Many were passengers who had already been up and dressed at the time of the collision, and who had arrived on the boat deck early. Among these were William Sloper and his bridge-playing companions, along with a number of the men from the smoking room. Lookouts Hogg and Jewell and Seaman William Weller were added to the lifeboat as crew.

"Are there any more ladies before this boat goes?" Murdoch called out. When none came forward he ordered the boat to be lowered away, and to wait by an after gangway to receive more passengers. It carried less than half its capacity of sixty-five.

As the block and tackle creaked, the men on deck began lowering boat No. 7. It gradually dropped past the A-deck promenade, the B-deck entrance doors and private promenade, a C-deck suite and the purser's office, and the reception room. On one side of the lifeboat the brilliantly lit decks glittered warmly, while on the other side the tranquil ocean stretched off into the darkness. When the boat finally touched the water it barely disturbed the glassy surface. It was 12:25 A.M., only three-quarters of an hour since the collision.

The evacuation of the *Titanic* had begun.

TOO FEW LIFEBOATS

No aspect of the *Titanic* tragedy provoked more outrage than the fact the ship carried lifeboats with a capacity for only slightly over half of the more than 2,200 people on board. Outdated British Board of Trade regulations for vessels of over 10,000 tons required a minimum of 16 lifeboats with a capacity of 5,500 cubic feet plus rafts and floats equal to 75 percent of the lifeboats' capacity. This meant that the 46,328-ton *Titanic,* which could carry a total of 3,511 passengers and crew, was required to carry boats for only 962 people. In fact, White Star had exceeded the regulations by including 4 collapsible boats, making room for 1,178.

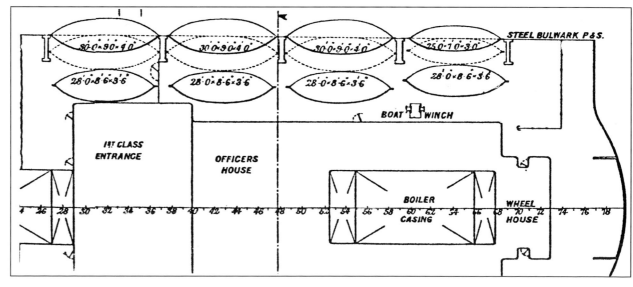

(Above) Shortly after leaving Southampton, the after boats were moved outboard, allowing for more deck space.

(Left) This painted brass plate in the shape of a White Star flag is from one of the Titanic's lifeboats.

One of the ironies regarding the Titanic's lifeboats is that her state-of-the-art Welin davits (above) were each designed to handle more than one lifeboat. As is shown by the diagram (right), the Titanic's sixteen regular boats could have been supplemented by an extra set inboard and even more by another two boats nested inside those sitting on deck, for a total of sixty-four. The need for so many boats apparently wasn't seriously considered — no one could imagine a situation where such a "watertight" ship would ever need to evacuate all of her passengers before help could arrive.

Chapter Five

TO THE LIFEBOATS

Monday, April 15, 12:40 A.M.

ALTHOUGH THE *TITANIC* NO LONGER needed steering, Fourth Officer Joseph Boxhall stood in the wheelhouse inside the bridge. For over forty-five minutes the ship had sat dead on the ocean, her forward compartments slowly filling with water as her bow sank lower and lower. Boxhall knew that this beautiful new ocean liner was doomed.

The wheelhouse telephone rang and Boxhall answered it immediately. It was Quartermaster George Rowe, keeping watch on the aft docking bridge. Rowe reported that he had just spotted a lifeboat in the water off the starboard side of the ship. Boxhall, who had heard no order for lifeboats to be launched, was surprised. He told Rowe to get some distress rockets and bring them to the bridge.

Meanwhile the aft well deck was becoming more crowded with steerage passengers, many of whom had found the path to the boat deck now blocked by closed doors or crewmen who would not allow them to enter the second- and first-class areas. Whether by accident or design, the first- and second-class passengers were being given the first chance to escape the sinking ship. More and more of these passengers now ventured out onto the boat deck, where a few officers and crew continued to work. First Officer Murdoch remained in charge of the odd-numbered starboard lifeboats, while Chief Officer Wilde had taken charge of preparing the even-numbered boats on the port side.

Working under Murdoch was Third Officer Herbert Pitman, who was now preparing boat No. 5 for lowering. As Pitman worked, Bruce Ismay stood nearby and watched impatiently. "There is no time to waste," Ismay finally announced, clearly implying that Pitman was moving too slowly. The officer did not recognize the managing director of the White Star Line and simply ignored the comment. Then, when the boat was swung out over the side into the ready position, Ismay again intervened, instructing Pitman to load it immediately with women and children.

"I await the commander's orders," Pitman replied abruptly.

"Very well," Ismay acknowledged.

Suddenly realizing that this gentleman matched a description he had been given of the White Star managing director, Pitman walked forward to the bridge, where Captain Smith was standing. Pitman informed the captain that a man he suspected of being Bruce Ismay wanted him to get the boat away.

"Go ahead, carry on," Smith replied.

Pitman promptly returned to boat No. 5, hopped in and called out, "Come along, ladies." Both men and women at first came forward and a number began climbing in. Ismay was nearby urging the Richard L. Beckwiths of New York and their party to climb into the boat. Mrs. Beckwith asked if they could all go.

"Of course, madam," he replied. "Every one of you." The Beckwiths, their daughter Helen Newsom, her fiancé, tennis star Karl Behr, and the Edwin Kimballs of Boston all climbed in.

"Are there any more women before this boat goes?" Ismay called out several times. Finally one came running up.

"Come along, jump in," he ordered.

"I am only a stewardess," she replied.

"Never mind," Ismay told her. "You are a woman. Take your place."

Pitman allowed a few more men in until the boat had over forty occupants. Its capacity was

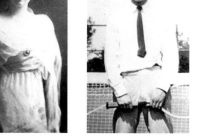

The second lifeboat to leave the Titanic *was No. 5. On board were first-class passengers Mr. and Mrs. Richard L. Beckwith of New York (top), their daughter Helen Newsom (above left), and American tennis star Karl Behr (above right).*

Lifeboat No. 7, the first one to depart, slowly creaks some fifty feet down the side of the Titanic *to the sea. Although the boat had a capacity of sixty-five, it carried only twenty-eight.*

sixty-five. He then jumped out to assist in lowering, leaving Quartermaster Alfred Olliver in command. At this point First Officer Murdoch approached and told him, "You go in charge of this boat and also look after the others. Stand by to come along the after gangway when hailed." The two shook hands. Murdoch added, "Good-bye. Good luck," as Pitman stepped into the boat. He didn't believe the ship would actually sink, but it suddenly struck him that the first officer did.

As boat No. 5 began to drop to the sea, someone on deck yelled down, "Be sure and see the plug is in that boat," referring to the hole that allowed water to drain from the lifeboats when they were stored on deck. Thomas Andrews' steward, Henry Etches, passed the word along to Olliver, who crawled around trying to find the plug for the bottom. Pitman blew his officer's whistle for the men to stop lowering the boat until they were certain the plug was in. From above, a voice called, "It is your own blooming business to see that the plug is in anyhow," and the lifeboat continued to descend. Olliver first pleaded with passengers to get out of his way, and finally pushed past them, forcing the plug in only after water had started to enter the boat.

As boat No. 5 settled on the sea, Anna Warren of Portland, Oregon, looked through the ship's portholes into the staterooms of

D-deck, the same deck where she and her husband had been sleeping a mere hour before, then high above the waterline, now almost at water level. Since the lifeboat was far from full, she assumed her husband had entered after assisting the other women, but now when she called his name there was no answer. The men rowed aft a short distance seeking the gangway Murdoch had ordered Pitman to come back to when hailed. The gangway was closed, so Pitman ordered the men to pull away from the ship.

While the first two lifeboats were being loaded and launched, in the wireless room Jack Phillips continued sending out distress messages that the *Titanic* was sinking and in need of immediate assistance. The word was soon spreading across the darkened ocean, and before long Phillips began receiving responses from other vessels. The first came from the German steamer *Frankfurt*, asking him to stand by, apparently while the operator informed his captain. Phillips sent Harold Bride to tell Captain Smith, whom Bride found on the starboard boat deck. Smith asked for the *Frankfurt*'s position, and Bride replied that they would get it as soon as possible.

By the time the junior operator returned, Phillips had heard from the Cunarder *Carpathia*, giving her position and saying she was coming hard. He again sent Bride to inform the captain. This time Bride found Smith in the wheelhouse, and the captain returned with him to the wireless room. He asked Phillips what other ships he had contacted, and was told the *Olympic*, the *Titanic*'s sister ship. Headed toward England, she was five hundred miles away

"What are you sending?" Smith asked.

"CQD," Phillips replied.

"Send SOS," Bride suggested. "It's the new call and it may be your last chance to send it." The operators chuckled, still finding it difficult to take the ship's plight seriously. After they had estimated the distance between the *Carpathia*

and the *Titanic*, Smith left without comment. The Cunard liner was roughly fifty-eight miles away, which meant it would take at least four hours to reach them.

So far only three ships had responded to the distress signal. The *Olympic* couldn't possibly arrive until sometime the next night. The *Frankfurt*'s signals seemed the strongest, but when she sent her position she proved to be over 170 miles away. Only the *Carpathia* was anywhere close. Could the *Titanic* last long enough not only for the Cunarder to reach her, but to conduct a successful rescue operation before the White Star liner went down?

As Phillips worked, he was having difficulty hearing communications from other ships, both because of the noise of the steam being vented off and because of a hissing noise that seemed to come from the ship's forward expansion joint right outside the cabin. It sounded as if air were escaping from below. A few moments later, Fourth Officer Boxhall brought a more accurate dead-reckoning position for the *Titanic* that he had worked up based on that evening's sights and an estimated speed of twenty-two knots. However, he could only place it on the table in front of the operators because conversation was too difficult. Boxhall had computed their position to be 41° 46' north, 50° 14' west. Phillips immediately sent out this position to the *Carpathia*.

On the port boat deck the work of readying the lifeboats for loading was progressing slowly. Chief Officer Wilde had ordered Second Officer Lightoller to uncover the boats but not to swing them out. Lightoller asked if all hands had been called, and Wilde replied that they had. The second officer then went to work on boat No. 4, and as each crewman appeared on deck he tapped him on the shoulder and gestured toward the boats. The roar of steam was too loud for spoken orders, but the men understood.

After confirming that the boats were being

THE VITAL ROLE OF WIRELESS

Although Guglielmo Marconi's invention had been in operation on board ships since the turn of the century, its use was far from universal in 1912. The *Titanic*'s wireless operators were Marconi Company employees and only indirectly responsible to the captain and his officers. Radio messages were very popular with passengers and were regarded as important navigational aids, but their use still lacked regulation. The *Titanic* tragedy highlighted this fact, since several ice warnings had been received but not reported to the bridge.

One of the first standard radio distress calls to be sent from a ship occurred in 1903 and was Marconi's newly created "CQD." "CQ" was the signal to stop transmission and pay attention; adding the "D" meant distress. In 1906 the International Radio Telegraphic Convention in Berlin created the signal "SOS" as an alternative means of summoning assistance. The three letters were chosen solely for their simplicity in Morse code. Three dots, three dashes and three dots were instantly recognizable, and could be transmitted by someone who had never before used a wireless apparatus. In 1908 "SOS" officially superseded "CQD"

as the regulation distress call, but Marconi operators rarely used the new signal. Only after Harold Bride radioed his now-famous SOS from the sinking *Titanic* did the new signal become standard.

In 1909 a distress call sent out on wireless was responsible for the incredible rescue of over sixteen hundred passengers and crew on board the White Star liner *Republic*. While the role of wireless in the rescue of the *Republic* made headlines, it was one ship's failure to use its wireless that stood out in the *Titanic* disaster. Had the *Californian* utilized her wireless to identify the mystery ship seen by her captain and officers, she would inevitably have heard the *Titanic*'s distress call.

After the *Titanic* disaster, ships were required to have a twenty-four-hour radio watch. More emphasis was placed on navigation, so that crucial information such as ice warnings would not go unreported to the bridge. Unfortunately, over fifteen hundred people had to die before the vital role of wireless was fully understood.

readied, Lightoller asked Wilde if they should swing out. "No, wait," the chief officer replied. Seeing the captain, Lightoller repeated his request. "Yes, swing out," Smith ordered. Wilde said nothing.

The second officer now had two men lower boat No. 4 level with the A-deck windows. Yet again Wilde held things up by refusing to allow Lightoller to load the boats, and again Lightoller approached the captain. "Yes," Smith replied. "Put the women and children in and lower away." Lightoller then ordered the passengers down to A-deck. Faced with Wilde's cautiousness and Smith's passivity, the second officer had clearly decided to take charge.

As the men worked, the deafening noise caused by the release of steam suddenly stopped, at last allowing the men to communicate more easily. Soon a very different sound could be heard as the bandsmen came up from the lounge, assembled on the deck, and began to play cheerful ragtime numbers.

On the bridge, Fourth Officer Boxhall waited impatiently for Quartermaster Rowe to arrive with the rockets. The reason for his impatience lay roughly ten miles away from the *Titanic* off the port bow. Once again he peered through his binoculars at the light that winked so tantalizingly. There was no doubt but that the flicker came from a steamer, and that she appeared to be approaching. First one and then two masthead lights were visible. Rescue was at hand! She was close enough, surely, to read a morse lamp. Boxhall immediately began signaling with a lamp from the port side of the bridge.

Seeing what his fourth officer was doing, Captain Smith approached. "Tell him to come at once," he ordered. "We are sinking." At one point Boxhall thought he had an answer, but when he repeated the message he could discern no response. Finally he concluded it was only the steamer's masthead light flickering.

Eventually Quartermaster Rowe reached the bridge with the rockets. "Fire one, and fire one every five or six minutes," Captain Smith ordered. It was 12:45, just over an hour since the *Titanic* had hit the iceberg.

"They wouldn't send those rockets unless it was the last," commented Emily Ryerson to her husband, Arthur. They were standing on the boat deck next to the officers' quarters when the first rocket rose with a rush of light and streaked into the sky above the masts and rigging, then burst into colored balls with a deafening boom.

"Can't you hear the band playing?" Arthur Ryerson asked in response, hoping that the music would lessen her fears. To Mrs. Walter Stephenson of Haverford, Pennsylvania, the sight of rockets could mean only one thing; the *Titanic* had been unable to summon help by wireless and this was the ship's last desperate attempt at communication. Soon all those on the boat deck realized that the *Titanic*'s situation was truly serious.

Yet the reassuring sight of the approaching steamer made it more difficult for Second Officer Lightoller to persuade the passengers to enter the boats. He was already having trouble convincing the women to part from their husbands. Captain Smith, who stood by the officers' quarters a few feet away, called out, "Women and children first." Lightoller repeated the words.

Gradually women began to enter lifeboat No. 6, just forward of the first-class Grand Staircase. The occupants were an unusual mixture, including a woman whose father was a United States congressman, the cashiers from the à la carte restaurant, a militant suffragette from England, and the daughter of the founder of the posh New York department store, Saks Fifth Avenue.

Fearing a shortage of capable hands, Lightoller was reluctant to place more than two crewmen in the boat — in this instance Frederick Fleet, the lookout who had spotted the iceberg,

and Quartermaster Robert Hichens, who had been at the wheel when the ship struck. He also hesitated to load the boat to capacity. Fully loaded each lifeboat weighed over 5 1/2 tons, and Lightoller was unaware that the new davits had been tested and could safely accommodate the weight. When less than two dozen women had entered the boat, which was capable of carrying sixty-five, he instructed Hichens, the senior crew member and therefore in charge, to pull for the nearby light, drop off the women and return for more passengers. He then ordered the crew at the davits to lower away.

Molly Brown had just finished persuading a Belgian woman to enter boat No. 6 rather than go below for her valuables. She was walking away to find out what was happening elsewhere on deck when a crewman grabbed her from behind. "You are going, too," he ordered, then picked her up and dropped her four feet into the lowering boat.

As boat No. 6 drew even with B-deck, Hichens suddenly realized he had only Frederick Fleet to row. "I can't manage this boat with only one seaman," he cried to those above. Lightoller had the men stop lowering as he tried to decide what to do. Not only could he not spare anyone, but the boat was now two decks below.

"If you like, I will go," came a voice from the crowd.

"Are you a seaman?" Lightoller asked.

"I am a yachtsman," Major Arthur Peuchen of Toronto replied, "and can handle a boat with an average man."

"If you are sailor enough to get out on that fall, you can go down," Lightoller told him.

Realizing how perilous such a descent would be for one of his passengers, Captain Smith suggested that Peuchen go below, break a window, and enter the boat through that. Peuchen replied he did not think that was feasible, and with that the Canadian major, three days short of his fifty-

(Above) Mrs. Margaret Brown, whose behavior in lifeboat No. 6 gained her fame and the nickname "The Unsinkable Molly Brown." (Right) It was a full hour after the Titanic *struck the iceberg that Captain Smith gave the order to send up the distress rockets. A ship visible off the port bow, however, showed no sign of responding.*

third birthday, swung hand over hand out onto the davit and climbed down the ropes into the waiting lifeboat.

Hichens ordered Peuchen to put the boat's plug in place, but in the dark Peuchen couldn't find it. He returned to where Hichens was waiting to release the falls once the boat hit the water and suggested the quartermaster put in the plug while he undid the shackles. When the plug was in, Hichens came rushing back to the stern. "Hurry up," he told Peuchen. "This boat is going to founder." At first Peuchen thought the plug hadn't been put in, but then realized Hichens was referring to the *Titanic*.

Apparently fearing that this "yachtsman" was trying to take charge, Hichens moved to assert his authority. "*I* am put here in charge of the boat. You go and do what you are told to do." Peuchen sat beside Fleet, each pulling an oar. While Hichens repeatedly ordered them to row hard to escape the suction of the liner, the two men's efforts gradually pulled the boat away in the direction of the distant light.

Down on C-deck Sarah Daniels approached the stateroom of the Hudson Allisons. She had disturbed Mr. Allison once and her employer was not likely to be pleased at being awakened a second time, but something was clearly very wrong with the *Titanic* and it was her duty to tell him. When Mr. Allison answered her knock she grabbed him by the arm, trying to convince him there was something seriously amiss. Instead he became cross with her for disturbing him and his wife. Chastened but determined, the maid returned to her cabin to dress. Her roommate, Alice Cleaver, was reluctant to wake the sleeping baby, Trevor, so Sarah quickly pulled a fur-lined overcoat over her clothing and left on her own.

As she hurried along the companionway she was met by a steward who immediately began fastening a lifebelt on her and told her to go on deck. When she protested that she wanted to go

back to warn the rest of her party, he assured her he would do so for her.

On the port side forward boat deck, women were being loaded into boat No. 8. Ida Straus, wife of the founder of Macy's Department Store, stepped forward with her maid, Ellen Bird. The young woman entered first, and Mrs. Straus passed a blanket to her. Then with one foot on the gunwale, the older woman changed her mind. She returned to her husband, Isidor, saying, "We have been living together for many years, and where you go, I go."

Friends of the couple were shocked, and they urged her to reconsider. "No," she replied firmly. "I will not be separated from my husband. As we have lived, so will we die together."

Hugh Woolner, a London businessman, appealed to Mr. Straus to enter the boat. "I am sure nobody would object to an old gentleman like you getting in. There seems to be room in this boat."

"I will not go before the other men," Straus replied firmly.

When Sarah Daniels stepped onto the deck a crewman grabbed her arm and hurried her to the side of boat No. 8. She tried to resist, protesting that she needed to alert the Allisons. "Never mind," he replied. "They will be looked after. Get in the boat. There is no danger, but we don't want to take any chances." Trusting his assurance that there was no real danger, Sarah allowed herself to be helped into the boat.

In all, only two dozen women entered the lifeboat, since Chief Officer Wilde now sent about twenty more women aft to boat No. 10. Second Officer Lightoller had again ordered only two crew members to man the lifeboat, but fearing a repeat of the situation at boat No. 6, Captain Smith ordered Steward Alfred Crawford and a cook to join them.

"Row straight for those ship's lights over there," Smith ordered Seaman Thomas Jones.

Major Arthur Peuchen (below), who belonged to the Royal Canadian Yacht Club in Toronto, was allowed to enter lifeboat No. 6 to help handle the boat. In 1987, an expedition that salvaged objects from the Titanic *wreck site recovered Major Peuchen's wallet, and in it was his calling card.*

(Right) Isidor Straus was returning with his wife, Ida, from a holiday at Cap Martin on the Riviera. A partner with R.H. Macy in the famous department store, he had also been elected to Congress and was a friend and confidant of President Grover Cleveland.

"Leave your passengers on board of her and return as soon as you can."

Once again a lifeboat left the ship far short of capacity.

At around 1:00 A.M. starboard lifeboat No. 3 left the ship with over forty people, including fifteen crew. Although five lifeboats now floated on the water and several others were in the process of being loaded, few passengers had yet grasped the desperateness of their situation. Word was still spreading that everyone was to put on their lifejackets and prepare to abandon ship. While some people, like the Hudson Allisons, still lay sleeping in their cabins, most now realized the ship was in trouble, but there was as yet no sign of panic. Many continued to place their hope in the nearby steamer, whose lights remained visible. Others assumed that many ships were racing to the rescue and would reach the scene long before a leviathan like the *Titanic* could possibly sink. And, although the incline of the deck was becoming more pronounced to some, the ship still seemed awfully safe and solid compared to the cold Atlantic. The lights still shone, the band still played, and the weather stayed calm.

Many crewmen reinforced the false sense of security, either deliberately or because they themselves couldn't believe the ship was sinking fast. Word spread among the passengers on the starboard boat deck that the *Titanic* couldn't sink in less than eight hours and that a number of steamers, including the *Olympic*, would be standing by within an hour or so. What a spectacular sight it would be to see the two sisters side by side on the calm ocean.

After boat No. 3 had been lowered, most of the passengers on the starboard boat deck moved aft. As a result, First Officer Murdoch found only a handful of crewmen nearby as he began loading boat No. 1, a smaller emergency boat. Sir Cosmo Duff Gordon approached with his wife, Lucile, and her secretary.

AND THE BAND PLAYED ON...

Mystery has long surrounded the exact role of the *Titanic*'s orchestra on the fateful night the ship sank. What did they play during those desperate hours, and when did they finally stop?

The ship actually had two small string ensembles. Five musicians, led by violinist Wallace Hartley, provided regular entertainment

for the first-class passengers, while three others played in the lounge outside the à la carte restaurant. One passenger remembers that they were wonderfully cooperative, playing any request from the White Star songbook (far right) which contained nearly 350 selections, spanning operas, waltzes, hymns, and rags.

After the collision, several uniformed musicians gathered together in the first-class lounge to entertain the passengers, beginning with ragtime and other cheerful numbers. Later they moved to the boat deck foyer and, finally, out onto the deck itself. Presumably the band grew larger as additional players arrived — it's unclear if all eight musicians played at any one time. Lawrence Beesley recalled seeing one of the cello players as late as 12:40 A.M. hurrying

(Above) A ship's orchestra of the period.
(Right) Seven of the eight Titanic *musicians with leader Wallace Hartley in the center.*

forward along the boat deck, the spike of his instrument dragging along the planking. This may have been Roger Bricoux, one of the French-born musicians. Survivor Bertha Lehmann recalled a French-speaking musician helping her on with her lifejacket and escorting her to the boats.

A number of passengers, including Edwina Troutt, later described hearing "Nearer My God to Thee" around the time the ship sank and it quickly became legend that this was the last tune the band played. Major Peuchen heard "Alexander's Ragtime Band" from boat No. 6. Harold Bride stated that the band had been playing ragtime until switching to "Autumn" just before the ship foundered. For a time it was thought that the Episcopal hymn by this name was played at the end, but Bride was probably referring to the waltz, "Songe d'Automne," then popular in British dance halls.

Romantic legend to the contrary, it seems most likely that the bandsmen eventually abandoned their instruments and attempted to save themselves. Sometime before the ship sank, Algernon H. Barkworth, an English justice of the peace, went below to retrieve some things from his room after hearing the musicians playing a waltz tune. Upon his return to the boat deck, the band had dispersed. Another survivor, Colonel Archibald Gracie, claimed to have witnessed the men set down their instruments a full half-hour before the *Titanic* foundered.

Whatever the exact sequence of events, there is no doubt that the bandsmen were heroes. There is no record of any one of them attempting to enter a lifeboat, and their efforts did indeed calm a number of passengers. Not one of them was saved.

"May we get into the boat?" he asked casually.

"Yes, I wish you would," Murdoch replied.

C.E. Henry Stengel, a New Jersey leather manufacturer, approached, irritated that the passengers were being inconvenienced and possibly endangered by being placed in lifeboats. When Murdoch told him to "Jump in!" his attitude changed and he obediently climbed to the rail and rolled into the boat. Murdoch laughed heartily. "That is the funniest sight I have seen tonight," he exclaimed. Stengel felt somewhat encouraged by the laughter. Perhaps the situation wasn't as dangerous as he had thought. The only other passenger to enter was Abraham Salomon of New York.

Murdoch now ordered a handful of crew members into the boat, including Lookout George Symons, whom he placed in charge, instructing him to stand off from the ship until called. As boat number No. 1 was lowered, it became caught on a guy wire at A-deck, but someone on the ship cut it away and they continued to the water. As the lifeboat pulled away from the *Titanic*, Symons could see that the D-deck portholes were awash, and the water was now just below the ship's name on the bow. It was far more apparent to him how far the ship had sunk than to those still aboard.

Once boat No. 1 had pulled well away from the ship, the men stopped rowing and rested. In a boat designed for forty, there were only twelve occupants. Of these, only five were passengers, and only two women.

For nearly an hour Minnie Coutts had sat patiently in her third-class cabin near the stern waiting for official instructions while her two sons continued to sleep peacefully in their bunks. The order to put on life preservers, when it finally came, presented her with a new problem; the cabin contained only two. Out in the hallway she discovered that other passengers were also short of lifebelts, and when she accosted a passing crewman he told her there were no more to be

had. In vain she kept asking anyone she saw.

Eventually the same crewman appeared in the now nearly empty hallway and when she again explained her predicament, he told her to follow him. With her two hastily dressed boys in tow, they set off down a network of corridors and through what Mrs. Coutts took to be first class until they reached his own quarters. Taking a belt, he fastened it on her, saying, "There! If the boat goes down, you'll remember me." She asked if there really was danger, and he replied yes, he was afraid there was. Before he left, he gave her directions to the boat deck.

Minnie Coutts and her two children headed for the boat deck, but when a door she was to take proved to be locked, she found herself lost in the bowels of the huge liner. She fought her rising panic at the prospect of being trapped in the sinking ship. Eleven-year-old Willie was himself nearly in tears when she made him promise that if she were to drown he would care for his little brother. Then, miraculously, another member of the crew happened along and showed them an alternate route to the boats.

Few in third class were as fortunate as Minnie Coutts and her two sons. To reach the boat deck they had to find their way through a veritable maze of third-, second-, and first-class corridors. To add to these difficulties, a number of crewmen were preventing men from leaving third class. The gates leading from the well deck had been locked, forcing a line of men to crawl along the jibs of the cargo cranes into second class, so they could reach the boat deck.

Most of the passengers on the well deck waited quietly, watching the lifeboats pulling away from the side of the ship, and the rockets bursting overhead. At one point an officer came and told the hundreds gathered there to be quiet because a ship was coming. Without any further word, the officer left.

Two of the Catholic priests from second class

LOWERING THE LIFEBOATS

After the disaster, the Titanic's sister ship, the Olympic, was fitted with additional boats. The photographs of her subsequent lifeboat tests (left and below) give a feeling for the scene on the Titanic's deck that night. (Right) An artist's rendering of the long descent from the boat deck exaggerates the distance but accurately conveys the sense of plunging into the unknown.

(Below) It seems unlikely that the rather well-bred passengers gathered on the A-deck promenade behaved in the overwrought fashion portrayed in this illustration of the time. Nonetheless, it was a scene of great emotion as fathers and husbands said farewell to their loved ones.

went down into third, circling among the passengers and offering comfort. A number of other steerage passengers gathered in the smoking room just aft of the well deck. Someone was found to play the piano, and a group began dancing. Others played cards and joked among themselves, trying to ignore the seriousness of the situation. For many it seemed best to keep their places and wait in their areas of the ship until they were told to do otherwise.

By around 1:20 A.M. six lifeboats had left the *Titanic*, none of them filled to capacity. On the starboard side where the aft boats were being quickly loaded, Kate Buss couldn't bring herself to look at them as she, Marion Wright, and Douglas Norman discussed their chances of being rescued. As they waited, another friend, Dr. Alfred Pain, joined them. Hearing a cry of "Any more ladies, this way," Pain and Norman rushed the two women to boat No. 9. As Miss Wright stepped across the gap between the rail and the frail-looking little boat, she didn't even say good-bye, assuming she'd be back soon. From the boat Kate Buss beckoned the two men to enter. Several other men from second class were already seated in their lifeboat, but when Norman moved to join them, crewmen held him back and the boat began to lower.

"Why didn't you let my friends come?" Miss Buss demanded of the man in charge. He replied that the order had been given to lower, and he would either do so or be shot and another man given his place. "And they would still not be allowed to come," he added.

WHILE THE SCENE ON THE BOAT DECK remained relatively calm, deep in the hull of the ship, where crewmen still toiled in boiler and engine rooms, the situation was quite different. These men risked their own safety to keep the lights burning and pumps working.

In boiler room No. 5, directly below the forward Grand Staircase, Engineer Jonathan Shepherd broke a leg when he stepped into an open manhole. While he lay in pain in the adjoining pump room, Engineer Herbert Harvey and Leading Stoker Fred Barrett continued working the pumps. Suddenly a huge wave of green foam came pouring from between the forward boilers, flooding the room. It was as if the entire bulkhead had disappeared.

Harvey ordered Barrett up an escape ladder while he ran for Shepherd. As Barrett began his climb, he saw the two engineers engulfed by water, but all he could do was to keep climbing.

When Steward F. Dent Ray ventured back to his room for an overcoat, he discovered that the water had reached E-deck in the forward part of the bow. The corridor was flooded almost as far as the main staircase. As the forward compartments filled with water and spilled over into those farther aft, the rate of sinking increased. The *Titanic* could not stay afloat much longer.

In his comfortable first-class cabin on C-deck, Hudson Allison had finally realized something was gravely wrong, and he went out to investigate. Leaving Alice Cleaver with his wife, Bess, and the two children, he headed for the upper decks.

Alice found Bess Allison nearly hysterical and trying to dress. She helped her employer put on a blouse and petticoat, then a fur coat. She then buttoned up her shoes and set out some brandy. Two-year-old Loraine and baby Trevor were still sleeping. Just as Mrs. Allison was beginning to calm down a little, a steward came by and ordered everyone up on deck. Now both women began to panic.

With Bess Allison once again verging on hysterics and still no sign of either Mr. Allison or Sarah Daniels, Alice was faced with rescuing a distraught mother and two tiny children all by herself. In fear for her own safety, she quickly grabbed a fur rug from Trevor's perambulator, wrapped it over the baby's nightgown, and announced to Mrs. Allison that she would not let the child out of her arms. Then, before the distraught mother could stop her, Alice took the baby and disappeared.

As Alice hurried along the hallway, she passed Mr. Allison on his way back to his stateroom. He seemed dazed, and was in such a rush that he

Ruth Becker and her brother, Richard.

looked right through the nurse and his child without recognizing them. Alice didn't pause or speak until she reached starboard boat No. 11. There she handed Trevor to Steward William Faulkner while she got into the boat. Because of the baby in his arms, Faulkner was also allowed into the boat.

Already on board were Mrs. Nellie Becker's two younger children, Marion and Richard. When the order was given to lower away, Mrs. Becker screamed, "Oh, please let me go with my

children," and jumped in. Suddenly she realized that twelve-year-old Ruth was still on the *Titanic*. "Ruth," she called to her daughter. "Get in another boat!"

As the lifeboat descended down the side of the ship, it became apparent to the crewmen on board that they had a problem: The boat would land dangerously close to the large rectangular opening for the condenser exhaust, now just above the waterline, from which a huge volume of water was pouring. As soon as the boat hit the surface, three men used oars to push the stern of the boat away from the waterfall while Steward Charles MacKay struggled desperately to release the after falls. It was fortunate they succeeded. There were seventy passengers in a boat designed for a maximum of sixty-five, and the gunwales were just inches above the water.

Just aft of the now empty davits for boat No. 11, men, women, and children climbed aboard boat No. 13 under Sixth Officer James Moody's charge. When Ruth Becker approached and asked if she could enter, Moody simply picked her up and dropped her in. Soon the boat was full. Moody had ordered the crew to begin lowering when two more women came rushing up followed by Albert and Sylvia Caldwell, teachers from a Christian college in Siam. As Mrs. Caldwell began to climb in near the center of the boat, someone tossed a small bundle Mr. Caldwell was carrying to Steward Ray at the stern. When Ray unrolled the blankets he discovered to his surprise that it was the Caldwells' ten-month-old son, Alden. Ray handed the baby to a woman nearby. Then just as the boat began to lower, Albert Caldwell climbed aboard near the bow.

Boat No. 13, now filled to capacity, began a shaky descent to the sea, tilting down at the bow one moment and the stern the next. Ruth Becker was too excited to feel afraid. Looking up, she saw that the decks above were crowded with faces. For all she knew, her boat and No. 15, the

WERE THEY KEPT BELOW?

Of the different classes of passengers, none sustained greater losses than third class; less than a quarter of these people were saved. Their terrible fate spawned the enduring legend that they were locked below, and that only the most resourceful managed to survive. But this was not the case.

Once word spread that the ship was sinking, several crewmen attempted to guide these mostly non-British immigrants to the boats. Pantryman Albert Pearcey stationed himself at a door leading from third to first class and directed the passengers up toward the boats. Steward John Hart found that the door connecting the third-class

Mr. and Mrs. Frederick Goodwin and all their children (above) were among those lost. (Right) This 1912 illustration demonstrates how challenging it could be to ascend from the lower decks of a sinking liner.

CROWS
NEST

BRIDGE

STARBOARD
BOATS

MAIN
STAIRCASE

WHEEL
HOUSE

FANS

OFFICERS' QUARTERS

FIRST CLASS GANGWAY
TO STAIRCASE & LIFTS

ELEVATOR

Do

Do

3rd CLASS
PROMENADE

Dd

STAIRS

CLOSED BULKHEAD (TO DIVIDE 1st
& 3rd CLASS)

DOOR

3rd CLASS
STAIRCASE

3rd CLASS PASSAGE

EMERGENCY DOOR
LEADING TO
MAIN
STAIRCASE

3rd CLASS
OPEN
SPACE

3rd CLASS PASSAGE

BULKHEAD
DOOR

STAIRS
TO

WATER LINE

3rd CLASS BUNK
OPEN FOR EMIGRANTS

STOKERS ESCAPING
SLAMMING DOWN DOORS
BEHIND THEM

DECK

HATCH

SQUASH
RACQUET
COURT

BULKHEAD
& WATER TIGHT
DOOR

BULKHEAD
WITH WATER
TIGHT DOOR

SPIRAL
STAIRCASE

MOTOR CARS

BOILERS

WATER
TIGHT
BULKHEAD

BULKHEAD

BOILERS

BAGGAGE
CARGO ETC

BOILERS

BULKHEAD

DOUBLE   BOTTOM

companionway to the second-class staircase had been opened, yet many passengers, unaware of this, rushed right past it and toward the stern. When he tried tying lifebelts on many of the people, some refused, insisting the ship wasn't damaged. At 12:30 A.M., after word arrived to pass the women from third class up to the boat deck, he had trouble finding any willing to go. Because many women refused to leave without their men, Steward Denton Cox guided both men and women to the boat deck.

Soon, however, access to the boat deck was restricted and other stewards prevented men from going up, although they still allowed women. The gates leading from the well deck to the second-class areas remained locked and some men were forced to crawl along the cranes to get to the higher decks. Although repeated attempts were made by the stewards to bring women from the well deck to the boats, it seems unlikely that anyone searched the corridors, cabins, and public rooms in third class. A high proportion of women and children in third class were lost, including all the large families on the *Titanic*. By the time the men were allowed up from the well deck, it was too late — most of the lifeboats had already gone.

119

last boats on the after starboard boat deck, were the last lifeboats on board. What was to become of all these people?

As No. 13 neared the water, Dr. Washington Dodge of San Francisco sought to free the oars to push the lifeboat away from the condenser exhaust, but found that the oars were lashed to the seats and that the people sitting on them were not inclined to move. Finally he and several others were able to get the oars free and push the bow away.

When boat No. 13 landed on the ocean's surface the force from the nearby exhaust water pushed it astern until the ropes still attached to the davits drew taut. The occupants found themselves directly beneath boat No. 15, which was now being lowered. In vain the crew on board sought to release the ropes, but they were so taut the mechanisms would not work. As No. 15 continued to descend, the occupants of No. 13 began calling desperately to those on deck to stop lowering, but their cries went either unheard or ignored. In No. 15 Fireman Frank Dymond recognized the voice of Fred Barrett, and he looked over the side to see No. 13 directly below. He joined in shouting to those on the boat deck.

Boat No. 15 loomed closer and closer. It was soon low enough for several of the men in the lower boat to press their hands against the bottom in a futile effort to push it away. Barrett jumped to the after falls with a knife while at the bow Seaman Robert Hopkins did the same. Hopkins called out, "One, two!" as he cut, and within seconds the ropes had been severed and boat No. 13 drifted out from under just before boat No. 15 landed.

Over on the port side Second Officer Lightoller continued to allow only women and children into the boats. He helped to maintain this policy by constantly assuring passengers that loading the boats was a precautionary measure, and explaining that the steamer still plainly

visible was only a few miles away.

At one point Chief Officer Wilde interrupted Lightoller's work to ask where the firearms were stored. These had been Lightoller's responsibility prior to the reshuffle at Southampton, where he had acted as first officer. Lightoller led Wilde, William Murdoch, and Captain Smith to the locker in Murdoch's cabin where the guns were kept. As the second officer turned to leave, Wilde

After lifeboat No. 13 had been lowered (above), water gushing from the condenser discharge caused it to float aft under boat No. 15, which was descending rapidly. At the last moment No. 13 was cut free and drifted to safety.

At twenty-eight, Fifth Officer Harold Lowe was one of the younger officers on board the Titanic *and this was his first trip across the Atlantic. He was off duty and fast asleep when the accident occurred and woke only when he heard voices outside his cabin. He then leaped out of bed, threw on his uniform, and hurried out on deck.*

shoved a revolver and some ammunition into his hand, saying, "Here you are. You may need it."

Lightoller slipped the gun into a pocket and hurried back to the boats. Passing Ida and Isidor Straus, he paused long enough to ask, "Can I take you along to the boats?"

"I think I'll stay here for the present," Mrs. Straus replied.

"Why don't you go along with him, dear," Mr. Straus suggested to his wife.

"No, not yet."

Eventually the couple moved off to some deck chairs and sat down together.

During the evening, Chief Baker Charles Joughin had periodically stopped by his cabin for a drink of whiskey. He was now so well fortified with alcohol that he hardly noticed the cold as he and several other crewmen forcibly hauled some women and children up from A-deck and began placing them in port side boat No. 10. He and his mates literally threw the children from the deck across a gap of several feet to the men in the boat. One of the last women to enter jumped and failed to clear the distance. Miraculously, Steward William Burke grabbed her ankle and prevented her from falling to the ocean. As he was about to pull her into the boat, someone on the open promenade deck just below reached out and grabbed her shoulders. For a few moments there was a human tug-of-war over the unfortunate woman hanging upside down more than sixty feet above the water. Eventually the man on A-deck won, and she was pulled back on board the ship.

Farther aft, as boat No. 14 became filled, Seaman Joseph Scarrott was forced to use the tiller to prevent men, whom he judged to be foreigners, from rushing in. None seemed to understand English and, after ordering one man out of the boat twice without success, he finally had to throw him out.

Fifth Officer Harold Lowe and Sixth Officer

Moody approached lifeboats Nos. 14 and 16 as people were still entering. Lowe remarked to Moody that he had seen five boats lowered, and that one of these next two ought to have an officer.

"You go," Moody told him. "I will get in another boat."

While Moody assisted with No. 16, Lowe finished loading No. 14. When Seaman Scarrott told him of the trouble he had experienced keeping men from rushing the boat, Lowe drew his revolver. He asked how many people were in the boat, and Scarrott replied that there were fifty-four women and four children.

"Do you think the boat will stand it?" the fifth officer asked, worried that it might buckle with the weight.

"She is hanging all right," Scarrott replied.

"All right. Lower away fourteen," Lowe ordered.

As lifeboat No. 14 began to drop, Lowe could see certain men in the crowd on deck who looked as if they were preparing to jump. Fearful that the sudden increase in weight might buckle the boat, he fired his revolver along the side of the ship. No one jumped.

As the boat neared the water, the aft end stopped while the bow continued to lower until it touched the ocean. The lifeboat now hung at a dangerous angle with the stern dangling five feet above the water. When Scarrott looked up toward the deck, he saw that the falls seemed to be twisted. Taking a knife from his pocket, he cut through the rope and the boat suddenly dropped onto the sea. When several women screamed, Lowe ordered, "Shut up," as Scarrott jumped to the plug. Fortunately it was in place.

By this time boat No. 16, which had been launched simultaneously, was pulling clear of the ship. Now No. 14 began to do the same. Soon the lifeboat's more than sixty passengers would begin to realize just how lucky they were to be free of the sinking *Titanic*.

WHAT HAPPENED THAT NIGHT

The many events that took place on the *Titanic*'s decks are condensed in time here to give a graphic overview of her final hours. The ship is depicted as she looked at approximately 1:30 A.M. on April 15, 1912 with her foc'sle awash. Major occurrences in the loading and lowering of lifeboats before and after that time are encapsulated to convey how and where the drama unfolded.

1 *Boats Nos. 5 and 7 were among the first to be lowered from the starboard side. Under the command of Third Officer Pitman, they would tie together during the night.*

2 *Boat No. 6, with Major Peuchen, Molly Brown, Lookout Frederick Fleet, and Quartermaster Hichens on board, rows away from the ship.*

3 *Boat No. 3 pulls away. The crewman at the tiller was so inexperienced he soon had the boat heading back to the sinking liner.*

4 *Boat No. 1, with a capacity of forty, has only twelve aboard including the Duff Gordons and seven crew.*

5 *The band plays on the deck near the first-class entrance on the port side.*

6 *Boat No. 8 carries twenty-eight people including the Countess of Rothes who eventually takes the tiller.*

7 *Carrying some fifty-six people, boat No. 9 pulls away from the starboard side.*

8 *Distress rockets are fired from the starboard bridge wing.*

9 *Boat No. 12, off the port side, carries forty women and children, and two seamen. By the time it reached the rescue ship, Carpathia, it would contain over seventy.*

10 *As No. 14 is loaded, a group of passengers appears ready to jump into the already full boat. Fifth Officer Lowe fires shots into the air to warn them away.*

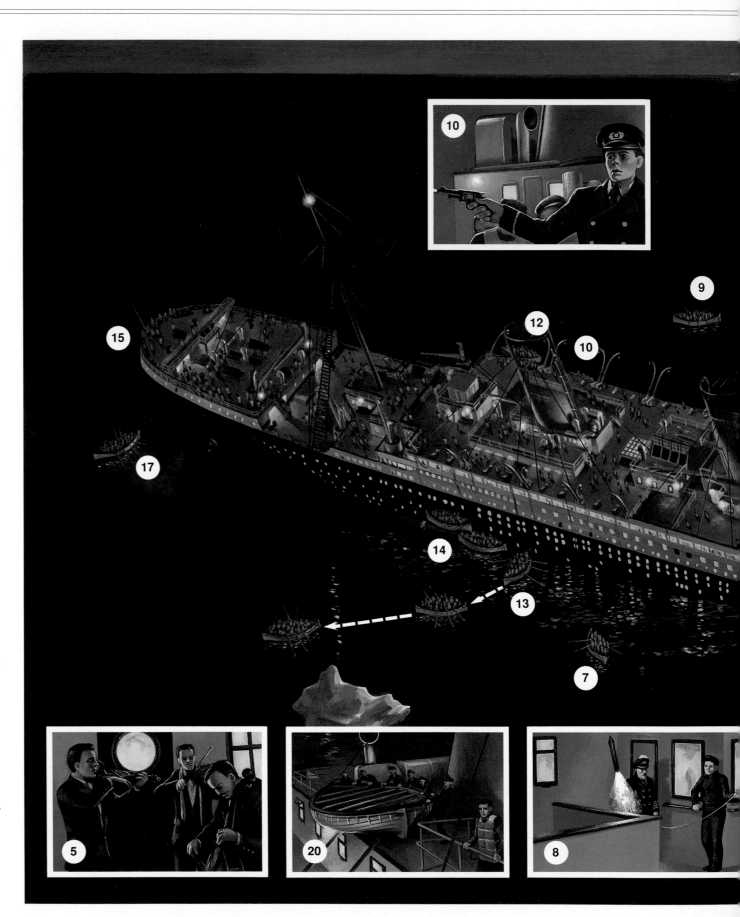

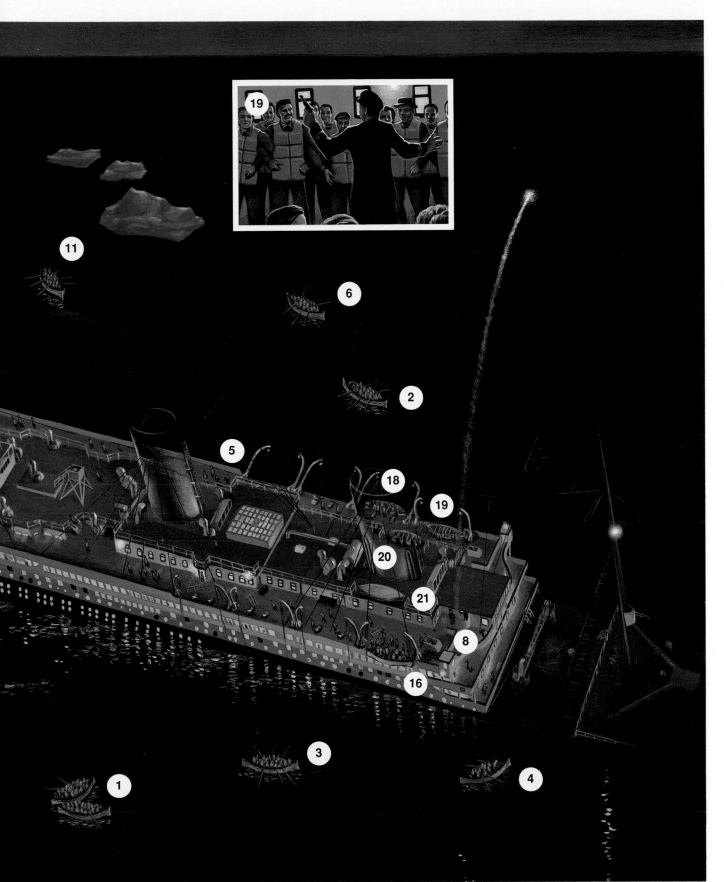

11 *Boat No. 10 pulls away from the port side. It will later tie up to boats Nos. 12 and 4, and collapsible D.*

12 *Boat No. 16 is made ready for lowering with an estimated fifty-six people on board.*

13 *The most crowded boat launched, No. 11 rows away from the ship with some seventy people.*

14 *With sixty-four people on board, No. 13 has just touched the sea. Water gushing from the condenser discharge has caused the boat to drift aft underneath No. 15 which is now being lowered on top of it. Crewmen in No. 13 manage to cut the falls and row the boat away with only moments to spare.*

15 *Passengers and crew continue to gather at the stern as it rises higher out of the water.*

16 *Collapsible C is lowered with thirty-nine people including Bruce Ismay, managing director of the White Star Line.*

17 *Boat No. 2, launched from the port side near the bridge, now pulls away at the stern. With a capacity of forty, it carries only twenty-five.*

18 *John Jacob Astor, refused entry to Boat No. 4, sees his wife off safely as she departs with other wealthy women and their maids.*

19 *Over 1,500 people are left on the sinking ship after 2:00 A.M. Collapsible D, with forty-four women and children on board, is ready for lowering. To prevent a rush on the boat, crewmen link arms and Second Officer Lightoller threatens the crowd with his revolver.*

20 *Crewmen struggle to free collapsible B from the roof of the officers' quarters. The boat fell to the deck and eventually floated off overturned, providing a refuge for some twenty-eight men who clung to it until rescued.*

21 *Collapsible A, also on the roof of the officers' quarters, was washed from the deck as the ship sank beneath it. Over a dozen people climbed into the swamped boat from the water.*

Chapter Six

DEATH OF A TITAN

KEN MARSCHALL 1982

Monday, April 15, 1:40 A.M.

T WAS NOW WELL PAST 1:30 A.M., AND FROM the fourteen lifeboats that had left the ship, the *Titanic* presented an incredible spectacle: the world's largest liner stopped dead and down dramatically at the bow, her huge propellers now looming out of the water. The forepeak was almost entirely submerged, yet many people had been unaware of the list while on board, and even now when viewing the ship from the boats were unconvinced she was doomed. The decks were still brightly lit, as was nearly every porthole. The strains of music still drifted across the placid surface, broken only occasionally by the hiss of a rocket shooting skyward, then bursting with an echoing boom. To Leading Stoker Fred Barrett, who had taken charge of boat No. 13, the *Titanic* looked like "a great lighted theatre" — an apt metaphor as one of the greatest dramas in the history of the sea entered its final act.

Although loaded to capacity, with the gunwales only inches above the water and the oars crossing and clashing, boat No. 13 managed to make progress in pulling away from the starboard side of the ship. Barrett, wearing only trousers and a light shirt and jacket, told those near him about the soup he had been warming on a piece of machinery at the time of the collision. "I could do with that hot soup now," he commented wryly as he shivered in the freezing air. Other firemen in the boat wore only short flannel pants and sleeveless shirts.

Ruth Becker, near the bow, suddenly realized she was still clutching several blankets her mother had sent her to retrieve from their cabin. They were soon being torn in half and distributed among the men. One crewman had somehow mangled his finger, which was now hanging by only a piece of flesh. In her coat pocket Ruth found a large handkerchief of her father's, which was soon wrapped around the injured man's hand.

On one side of Ruth a woman was sobbing. When the girl questioned her, the woman replied in a language Ruth didn't understand. "She is speaking German," a tall man on her other side volunteered. With him as interpreter, Ruth learned that, like her, this woman had been separated from her family at boat No. 11. Her tiny baby had been placed on board, and then the boat was lowered away before she was allowed to enter. She feared that someone in the other boat, not realizing the well-wrapped bundle was an infant, would throw it overboard. Ruth, sounding more like an adult than a twelve-year-old, promised the woman she would help her find the baby when they were rescued.

At the other end of boat No. 13 the woman holding ten-month-old Alden Caldwell was distributing spare wraps to people around her. She offered one to Leading Stoker Barrett, but he declined as there were still women not fully clad. Suddenly the baby began to cry. She turned to Lawrence Beesley beside her and asked, "Will you feel down and see if the baby's feet are out of the blanket? I don't know much about babies, but I think their feet must be kept warm."

Beesley found that the child's toes were exposed, and as soon as he wrapped them up again the crying stopped. It was too dark to see faces, but Beesley thought he recognized the woman's voice as one of his companions at the assistant purser's table. "Surely you are Miss Slayter?" he asked.

"Yes," Hilda Slayter replied, "and you must be Mr. Beesley. How curious we should find ourselves in the same boat!" The two soon discovered that although he was from England and she from Halifax, Nova Scotia, they had a mutual

Schoolteacher Lawrence Beesley (above) boarded boat No. 13 with his dressing gown, which he had been carrying over his arm since leaving his room. He later wrote a vivid account of the sinking. (Right) Just after 2:00 A.M. the Titanic's stern had lifted far enough out of the water to expose her giant propellers. The occupants of boat No. 16 watch as lifeboat No. 14 makes the perilous descent to the water.

acquaintance in Clonmel, Ireland.

Lifeboat No. 6, under the command of Quartermaster Robert Hichens, made little progress in pulling away from the liner with only Major Peuchen and Frederick Fleet at the oars. Almost immediately after the boat was launched, a young steerage passenger made an appearance, having apparently stowed away while the boat was still on deck. He was put to work at an oar only long enough for the others to discover that he had an injured arm. The oar was then pulled back in. Major Peuchen asked Hichens to give one of the women the tiller so he could join the rowers, but Hichens refused. He seemed threatened by Peuchen's military bearing and knowledge of boats, announcing that he was in command and it was Peuchen's job to row.

When an officer's whistle sounded from the *Titanic*, summoning boat No. 6 to return, Hichens ordered the two men to stop rowing while he listened. The boat's occupants could hear Captain Smith shout, "Come alongside," and Hichens debated whether or not to obey. Several of the women reminded him that the captain's parting orders had been to row for the light in the distance. Finally the quartermaster decided it would be safer to pull away. "No, we are not going back to the boat," he remarked. "It is our lives now, not theirs."

As boat No. 6 continued to creep along, Molly

Brown decided that the men needed help at the oars. She placed one in an oarlock and asked Margaret Martin of the ship's restaurant to hold it while she placed another in an oarlock on the other side. To her surprise, Miss Martin began rowing very effectively, and the two were soon pulling side by side. Other women quickly joined them, while Hichens launched into a tirade about how the suction of the sinking *Titanic* would draw under everything for miles around. As proof he recalled the incident with the S.S. *New York* in Southampton. When the *Titanic* sank, he added, her boilers would surely explode. Whenever the ladies seemed to tire, Hichens would repeat his grim predictions.

(Above) The final moments of the sinking as depicted by an artist for the Sphere.

(Left) Although Captain Smith called through a megaphone ordering several boats to return to pick up more passengers, none responded until after the ship had gone down, fearing they would be swamped.

(Right) From the A-deck promenade, women of wealth and social prominence as well as poor immigrants enter a lifeboat.

Those on board the *Titanic* watched as the procession of boats pulled away from the ship's side. Some disappeared into the darkness, while others were still visible several hundred yards away. Occasionally Captain Smith attempted to hail them through a megaphone, ordering the partially filled ones to return, but none responded. Only lifeboats Nos. 2 and 4 and the four collapsibles remained on board to evacuate 1,700 passengers and crew. Yet many still hesitated. Thomas Andrews, who had spent much of the time opening staterooms searching for passengers, was appalled at how many women were still reluctant to get into the lifeboats. "Ladies, you must get in at once!" he cried as the last boats were being loaded. "There is not a minute to lose. You cannot pick and choose your boat. Don't hesitate. Get in. Get in!"

Wearing their life preservers, the bandsmen continued to play, having long since abandoned ragtime and lively numbers for waltzes and other quieter pieces. Many people would later claim that the band played "Nearer My God to Thee." Winnie Troutt, forward on the port side, also recognized Elgar's "Land of Hope and Glory."

In the wireless room Harold Bride had been keeping up the wireless log while Jack Phillips worked the key. Periodically Bride left to report their work to the captain, and occasionally Smith would stop in personally to check on them. During one visit he told them the engine room was flooded, the ship was sinking, and that she could not last longer than half an hour. Phillips passed along the news to the *Carpathia*, now fully aware that the Cunarder could not possibly reach them in time.

Finally Jack Phillips decided to go out to have a look around and Harold Bride took over the key. He got in touch with the *Baltic*, but the signal was so unsatisfactory he decided the steamer was too far away to be of assistance. He signaled that they were sinking fast and that there was no hope of saving the ship.

Phillips returned and reported that the forward well deck was awash and that things looked "queer." He suggested the two of them put on more clothing and their lifebelts. While Bride prepared to leave, Phillips sat back down at the key and called "CQD" once more.

For over an hour some of the elite of New York and Philadelphia society had waited to get into boat No. 4. Second Officer Lightoller had sent them down to the A-deck promenade, planning to load the boat from there, but when he found the windows closed he had gone on to other boats and the passengers had returned to the boat deck. Some had left in other boats. Now the Astors, Wideners, Carters, Thayers, and Ryersons along with assorted servants were led back down to A-deck by Chief Second Steward George Dodd. By now the windows had been opened and Lightoller had placed deck chairs up against the rail to act as steps.

As the lifeboat began to load, Dodd noticed young John Ryerson among them.

"That boy can't go!" Dodd announced, putting his hand in front of the teenager to prevent him from approaching the boat. Arthur Ryerson stepped forward.

"Of course that boy goes with his mother," he insisted. "He is only thirteen."

"Very well, sir," Dodd agreed, "but no more boys."

Lucile Carter, hearing Dodd's remark, rushed up to her own thirteen-year-old son and placed her hat on his head. Dodd made no attempt to prevent the younger Carter from getting on the boat.

Colonel Archibald Gracie gently lifted pregnant Madeleine Astor and passed her to Lightoller. Colonel Astor leaned out one of the windows and asked if he could go with his wife to protect her. "No, sir," Lightoller replied. "No men are allowed in these boats until women are loaded first." Lightoller still refused to waver on the unwritten law of the sea. Astor asked the number of the boat in order to locate his wife later, and then tossed his gloves to her. Lightoller was certain Astor wanted the number in order to lodge a complaint, but he felt confident that he had done the right thing.

When boat No. 4 was finally loaded with women and children, Lightoller ordered it lowered. Emily Ryerson was shocked when they reached the water only a few feet below. The C-deck portholes were quickly disappearing beneath the surface. Many were open, and the water was pouring through them into the ship.

As boat No. 4 pulled away, Emily Ryerson saw that the larger, rectangular B-deck windows were soon awash. The staterooms were brilliantly lit, and she watched as the water cascaded through the open ports and flooded around the furniture. A few feet from her, Quartermaster Walter Perkis, in charge of the boat, was unconcernedly smoking a pipe.

"What were your orders?" Mrs. Ryerson demanded.

"There is another companionway aft, and we are ordered to go there," he replied.

Several of the women balked at the idea. "Don't go," one cried. "The ship is going down and we will be swamped."

Undaunted, Perkis ordered the men to pull for the stern. The water alongside the ship was now littered with deck chairs, casks and even doors that were being thrown from on board. From inside the *Titanic* came a cracking noise like china breaking. There was no open gangway to be seen.

From the stern boat deck, where about twenty firemen had congregated, Greaser Thomas Ranger watched boat No. 4 approach. Seizing the opportunity, he and Greaser Fred Scott climbed out onto boat No. 16's empty davits and worked their way down the falls. Despite the difficulty of

Among the wealthy passengers who entered boat No. 4 were Lucile Carter (top), her two children, Lucile and William (above middle), and Madeleine Astor (above). (Right) Boat No. 4, being loaded by Second Officer Lightoller through the windows of the A-deck promenade, is nearly ready for launching, while a crowd begins to gather on the boat deck at collapsible D. The occupants of boat No. 6 stare in amazement as water pours through the open ports on D-deck.

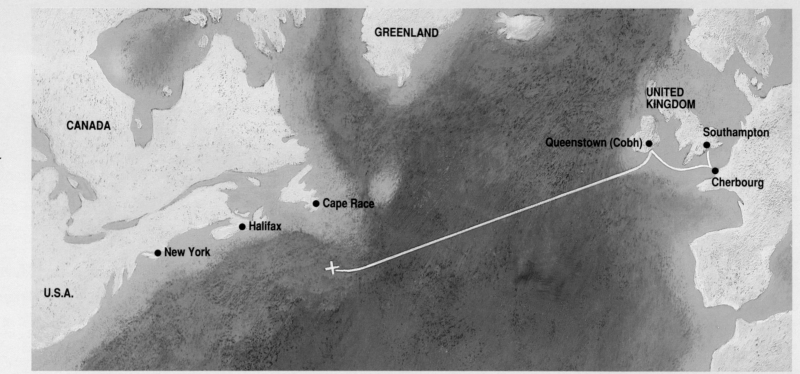

The path of the *Titanic* from Southampton to where she collided with the iceberg approximately 400 miles off the coast of Newfoundland. From the discovery of the *Titanic* wreck we now know that the ship was actually 13.5 miles east-southeast of her estimated distress position.

climbing while wearing a lifebelt, Ranger successfully dropped into lifeboat No. 4. Scott fell into the water, but was quickly hauled aboard by the women.

IT WAS NOW NEARLY 2:00 A.M. THE *TITANIC*'S last rockets had been fired, and all but collapsible boats C and D had left the ship. Collapsibles A and B were still lashed upside down to the roof of the officers' quarters. Collapsible C would get away first. When some men climbed aboard, Purser Herbert McElroy fired his pistol into the air, and several male passengers on the *Titanic* hauled the interlopers out. The boat was then filled with women and children.

Just as the collapsible was being lowered, two gentlemen stepped on board. One was William Carter, whose wife and son had left a few minutes earlier on boat No. 4. The other was Bruce Ismay. Until now Ismay had patrolled the boat deck, giving orders to the crew and overseeing the loading of the boats. With the *Titanic* clearly close to sinking, he had decided to save himself.

Second Officer Lightoller was preparing to load collapsible D from the port side where it had been fitted into the forward davits used by lifeboat No. 2. The *Titanic*'s bow was down so far that the water was only ten feet below the boat deck. Even now, with the ship nearly gone, Lightoller held to the strict code of "women and children first." When several men tried to rush the boat, he drew the gun from his pocket.

The second officer would later tell Colonel Gracie that he had to fire his revolver to make the men get out, although he formally testified at the British inquiry that there was perfect order and no rushing at the boat. Years later, in his autobiography, Lightoller would admit to having had to brandish an "unloaded" revolver to persuade the men to leave the collapsible. Whatever the truth, the men backed off. The crew then formed a ring around the area through which only women could pass.

(Above) Colonel Archibald Gracie later wrote a well-regarded account of the Titanic *disaster, but died before it was published.*

132

Winnie Troutt had watched the loading and launching of the final boats with a kind of emotionless detachment. She had long since given up any idea of being saved. Too many husbands and wives had been separated that night, and she thought it "wicked" to save single girls such as herself at the expense of men with wives and families. She did not want to be responsible for the loss of other lives, and she intended to stay aboard the ship, grateful that the Lord was to spare her family the cost of a funeral.

Suddenly a man holding a baby approached. "I don't want to be saved," he cried, "but who'll save this baby?" The young woman accepted the child. Now she had a reason to be rescued. She made her way toward collapsible D.

As Winnie Troutt neared the ring of crewmen guarding the boat, another woman scoffed, "Oh, you're foolish," when she saw that Miss Troutt had taken the responsibility of caring for a baby when the ship was so near to sinking.

"Why, you nasty thing!" Miss Troutt snapped back angrily. Then she turned to a crewman and asked, "What will become of us?"

"Oh, don't worry, mum," he replied. "The White Star Line will take care of you both." Winnie Troutt was then hustled into the boat and the baby was passed to her.

While the last boat was being loaded, Colonel Gracie and his friend, J. Clinch Smith, had been running along the boat deck shouting, "Are there any more women?" Now they heard Lightoller call out, "All passengers to the starboard side!" Perhaps Lightoller hoped to correct the ship's list to port, which was making it difficult to lower the boat, or more likely he simply wanted to keep the crowd away. Gracie and his friend followed the second officer's order and joined the crowd heading to starboard.

A group of people had congregated along the midship rail aft of where boat No. 7 had been, and among them Colonel Gracie recognized John Thayer and George Widener, two of the wealthiest men on board, looking over the side and talking earnestly. Next to them, to Gracie's horror, he saw Caroline Brown and Edith Evans, two women he had escorted to the boats an hour and a half earlier. As Mrs. Brown began describing how she and Miss Evans had become separated from her two sisters, a crewman came along saying there was room for more ladies in the boat on the port side. Gracie seized the two by the arm, and with Miss Evans on his right and Mrs. Brown on his left he ran toward collapsible D, several other women following.

When Gracie neared the lifeboat, he was stopped by the ring of crewmen. The women proceeded alone, but when they were about to enter Edith Evans turned to Caroline Brown and said, "You go first. You are married and have children." She assisted the older lady over the rail, and then, instead of following, called out, "Never mind. I will go on a later boat." With that, the younger woman turned and hurried away along the deck.

Finally Chief Officer Wilde felt he could wait no longer to launch collapsible D. The ship was too close to foundering. "You go with her, Lightoller," he told the second officer, who was then standing in the boat to help women board.

"Not damn likely," Lightoller replied, jumping back on deck to man the after fall. To the end Lightoller's behavior could only be described as "by the book."

(Above) Sometime after 1:00 A.M., passengers hurriedly ascending the first-class staircase on their way to the lifeboats notice that water is now flooding the E-deck landing, five decks below.

First-class passengers Hugh Woolner and Bjornstrom Steffanson had gone down to A-deck after seeing collapsible C safely loaded and launched. There was no one the length of the deck, and the lights were beginning to glow red as the power waned. As the men stood near the bow, water suddenly began pouring over the rail at the forward end of the deck. They jumped to the rail along the side of the ship where collapsible D was being lowered just a few feet away.

"There is nobody in the bow," Woolner cried. "Let's make a jump for it. You go first."

"Right you are," Steffanson replied, and he jumped for the boat, landing head over heels in the bow. A moment later Woolner jumped, but he was not so lucky. His cork life preserver bounced him off the gunwale, but he managed to catch the edge of the boat with his fingers while his legs dropped into the sea. As he managed to hook his right foot over the gunwale, Steffanson helped him in, and a moment later the boat touched the water.

THE *TITANIC'S* ENTIRE BOW WAS NOW WELL submerged, with her mast and rigging rising from the sea. The lights still shone, though less brightly. Most of the remaining steerage passengers and crew had retreated to the stern, with the first- and second-class staying on the boat deck. A small crowd of men swarmed over the roof of the officers' quarters where the two remaining collapsible boats were still securely lashed.

Elsewhere other men prepared for the ship to founder. Chief Baker Charles Joughin, with remarkable clarity of mind considering all the liquor he had drunk, took about fifty deck chairs from the A-deck promenade and threw them overboard one at a time. He hoped swimmers would be able to cling to them. One of the passengers opened up the kennels on the boat deck, freeing the dogs that had been housed there.

First-class passengers Norris Williams and his father, Duane, wandered about, dropping down to A-deck to view the large map where the ship's run had been posted each day. What good had the impressive runs done them, the younger Williams wondered.

When Williams and his father returned to the boat deck they could see the lights of some of the lifeboats in the darkness. The water sparkled like light reflected through a prism. They could feel the ship sinking more rapidly beneath them.

The extreme cold forced Williams and his father into the gymnasium where in spite of the ship's sharp slope they rode the stationary bicycles. Nearby, Instructor T.W. McCawley was still at his post, talking with others who had also gathered there.

At the extreme aft end of the poop deck, Storekeeper Frank Prentice stood chatting and smoking with several of his mates. Everyone seemed calm, and from somewhere Prentice could hear what sounded like a large group of people singing hymns. Trimmer Thomas Dillon had been waiting there almost an hour for the ship to go down. He could see no women among the passengers, and the men were behaving in a very orderly fashion.

Someone had finally come to the aft well deck and told the third-class men waiting there that they could go up to the boat deck. It seemed pointless now, and most preferred to stay. Three Norwegians — twenty-six-year-old Olaus Abelseth, his cousin Peter Sjöholt, and Sigurd Moen his brother-in-law — did decide to take their chances on the boat deck. Even there they chose to stay aft on higher ground and avoid the crowd struggling to prepare the last two collapsibles.

At one point a crewman came near where Abelseth and his relatives stood. "Are there any sailors here?" he called. Although Abelseth had

Tennis star Norris Williams (below left) was one of the passengers who rode the stationary bicycles (below right) in the gymnasium to pass the time as the ship was sinking.

In a photograph taken at Queenstown, instructor T.W. McCawley demonstrates one of the gymnasium's rowing machines. Behind him, electrician Henry Parr sits astride a mechanical horse.

As the Titanic *plunges downwards at around 2:15 A.M., water comes crushing through the wrought-iron and glass dome over the first-class staircase and rushes down the stairs past the clock depicting Honor and Glory crowning Time.*

earned his living as a fisherman, his two companions persuaded him to remain with them, admitting they could not swim.

In the wireless room, with the lights growing dim, Jack Phillips still worked the key. While he did so, Harold Bride helped him on with his overcoat and lifejacket. When the captain entered, Bride noticed that Smith still had not put on his own life preserver.

"Men, you have done your full duty," Smith told them. "You can do no more. Abandon your cabin." They didn't move. "You look out for yourselves," the captain continued. "I release you. That's the way of it at this kind of time. Every man for himself."

Once Captain Smith had gone, Phillips went back to his key. Bride was moved by the way Phillips remained at his post while the ship was about to sink under him. He stepped into their sleeping quarters to pocket his spare money, and when he returned he found a stoker stealthily removing Phillips' lifebelt. As Bride grabbed the man, Phillips jumped to his feet, and a scuffle ensued. Finally Bride got a hold on the crewman,

Although her bow is now fully submerged, the lights on the Titanic *still cast a glow over the water. Those in the nearby lifeboats hear an ever-increasing roar as everything movable in the ship — from five grand pianos and dozens of carefully packed trunks to thousands of pieces of silver and china — crashes forward.*

allowing Phillips to swing at him until he collapsed to the floor. From forward they could hear water pouring onto the bridge.

"Come, let's clear out," Phillips called. Leaving the stoker to his fate, the two men ran from the cabin. Then they climbed to the roof of the officers' quarters, where Bride went to work helping to free collapsible B.

On the starboard side several oars had been leaned up against the deck house so the men could slide collapsible A down to the boat deck. But they had underestimated the weight of the boat and overestimated the strength of the oars. As the men pushed the collapsible from the roof it crashed to the boat deck. It was upright, however, and despite Sixth Officer Moody's desire to float it from the deck, the men began attaching it to the falls of the nearby davit. As they worked, Captain Smith approached with a megaphone and shouted to those on deck, "Well, boys, do your best for the women and children, and look out for yourselves."

Over on the port side, collapsible B landed upside down on the boat deck. Suddenly there came a gurgling noise as water began pouring over the forward railings onto the bridge and up through the hatchways behind the bridge wings that led to A-deck. Now the bow of the *Titanic* began to plunge swiftly, causing a huge wave to wash aft from the forward end of the boat deck.

The moment Captain Smith had feared was at hand — the ignominious end to a previously untarnished career. During the two and a half hours since the collision, he had at times seemed almost in a daze, a strangely passive figure. Fourth Officer Boxhall was the one who had taken the initiative to find the rockets and try to signal the mysterious steamer that still lay tantalizingly in sight. And the launching of the lifeboats would have been delayed even longer had Second Officer Lightoller and Third Officer Pitman not approached the captain for permission to load

and lower them.

Now, with his ship going down, Captain Smith turned and dived into the ocean.

The men near the overturned collapsible B clambered over it as it was washed from the deck. On the starboard side Steward Edward Brown cut the after falls of collapsible A and called out for someone to cut the forward ones as people scrambled on board. Several passengers loosened them before the wave washed most of the occupants out. The boat slammed into a davit, then drifted against the forward funnel as the bridge disappeared under water, before finally floating away with only a few occupants remaining.

The wave washed many people overboard, among them Assistant Cook John Collins and a steward, each carrying one of a sobbing woman's two small children toward collapsible A. As the wave engulfed them, the infant in Collins' arms was swept away along with its mother, the steward, and the other child.

Colonel Gracie and Clinch Smith had been heading aft when a crowd of people suddenly began pouring from the first-class entrance, many women among them. At the sight of the advancing water, the crowd turned and attempted to run aft, only to be blocked by the railing that divided the first-class and engineers' promenade areas. Gracie and Smith both jumped for the roof of the officers' quarters and fell back, but as Gracie came down, the advancing water hit his right side. He jumped again, rising with the wave, and was able to haul himself onto the roof. But when he looked for his friend, whom he had promised to stick by no matter what happened, Smith was gone. A moment later Gracie was dragged under as the bow continued to dive, and he found himself spinning in a whirlpool. Far beneath the surface, he struggled to swim away.

With a rumbling, crashing noise the stern gradually rose into the air while the forward half of the *Titanic* sank even more. Charles Lightoller had simply walked into the water from the roof of the bridge and, seeing the crow's nest directly ahead, he instinctively began swimming toward it. Just as he realized how useless this was, he was sucked against a ventilator. Each time he struggled to get free, he was drawn back by the rush of water pouring down it.

Farther aft A.H. Barkworth, an English justice of the peace, was nearly caught in the crowd as people attempted to climb for the stern. Someone screamed, "Go gently!" as if their motion might upset the ship. Barkworth flung his briefcase overboard and climbed the rail. The water was too full of debris to dive safely, so he stepped off and dropped down the side of the ship.

With a great tearing of metal, the forward funnel of the ship suddenly toppled toward the bow. As it crashed down onto the water, emitting a cloud of sparks and soot, it created a wave that washed everyone off overturned collapsible B and swept the boat twenty feet clear of the ship. Lightoller, freed from the ventilator by a blast of hot air from below, now clung to this boat by a rope. Norris Williams somehow escaped being crushed by a matter of inches, but his father beside him was killed.

By now the deck was so steep that people were literally sliding off it into the water. Those in the lifeboats still near enough to watch the final minutes of the tragedy unfold would never forget the experience. In boat No. 13 Ruth Becker could hear screaming and watched as people jumped from the ship. Bruce Ismay in collapsible C turned his back. He could not look at his great ship as it sank.

It sounded as if everything loose inside the ship were crashing and breaking. The lights, which had somehow remained lit until now, went out all at once, plunging the ocean into darkness and leaving the *Titanic* visible to those in the more distant boats as only a dark outline in the starry sky.

Suddenly the great ship began to split between the third and fourth funnels. In boat No. 5 Elmer Taylor recognized instantly what was happening. "The cracking sound," he wrote later, "quite audible a quarter of a mile away, was due, in my opinion, to tearing the ship's plates apart, or that part of the hull below the expansion joints, thus breaking the back at a point almost mid-way the length of the ship."

As the *Titanic* broke in two, the bow slid below the surface and the stern settled back momentarily, almost to an even keel. Within seconds it too began to sink, the broken end going under and the aft section rising higher and higher until it was nearly perpendicular to the water. In the water nearby, Jack Thayer, Jr., rather than try to swim away, allowed his lifebelt to keep him afloat as he watched, fascinated, oblivious to the cold. The people still on board were clinging like bees to benches, railings, ventilators — anything that would support them. Occasionally some would fall, either in groups, pairs, or singly.

Eugene Daly of Athlone, Ireland, having climbed aboard collapsible B, feared the ship would topple over onto his boat at any second. In collapsible D, Hugh Woolner fixed his attention on a single porthole near the water. It did not move. The *Titanic* was no longer sinking.

Standing on the very stern, Storekeepers Frank Prentice, M. Kieran, and Cyril Ricks had felt the ship rumbling as the stern climbed higher. Now they decided it was time to jump. Ricks went first, followed by Prentice, who dropped past the propellers and, finally, when he thought he would never reach the water, plunged into the sea. The icy Atlantic, three degrees below freezing, cut him like a knife. Nearby Ricks floated unconscious. He had apparently struck something. The sea about them was strewn with wreckage.

The stern section of the ship remained vertical and motionless for what was estimated at anywhere between thirty seconds and several minutes, then began to plunge, picking up speed as it went.

As horrified passengers watch from lifeboats, the Titanic *splits in two between the third and fourth funnels. The ship tore apart where several large open spaces within the hull produced a natural weak spot.*

Standing on the very stern, Chief Baker Charles Joughin felt as if he were riding an elevator. As the ship went under he simply stepped into the water and paddled away without even getting his head wet.

Just as the *Titanic*'s stern disappeared, four final reports, sounding to Herbert Pitman in boat No. 5 like gunshots, emanated from the wreck.

It was 2:20 A.M. "She's gone, lads," a crewman announced in boat No. 3. "Row like hell or we'll get the devil of a swell." In No. 4, closer to the scene, a crewman cried out, "Pull for your lives or you'll be sucked under!" Ladies such as Madeleine Astor and Marian Thayer grabbed oars and helped the crewmen row away. Now the tiny lifeboats lay scattered on an empty ocean.

Chapter Seven

RESCUE

Monday, April 15, 2:30 A.M.

CAPTAIN ARTHUR ROSTRON STOOD ON the bridge of the 13,600-ton Cunard liner *Carpathia* and stared into the clear moonless night. Unknown to his ship's 750 passengers sleeping peacefully in their cabins, a pleasant springtime cruise to the Mediterranean was abruptly turning into a desperate rescue mission. Rostron knew that ahead of him in the darkness lay icebergs, but he had to risk going at top speed. Too many lives were at stake. He had taken what precautions he could, posting two additional lookouts on the bow to watch for ice and instructing his second officer, James Bisset, to stand sentinel on the starboard bridge wing. Later Bisset remembered how his face stung as the frigid night air rushed past him. He also remembered glancing over at the bridge where the captain, standing alone, bowed his head for a moment of prayer.

There was nothing more Rostron could do but wait and hope. A twenty-seven-year veteran of the sea who had served as chief officer aboard the *Lusitania*, the forty-three-year-old captain acted decisively and swiftly as soon as he received the *Titanic*'s call for help. He ordered the ship's three doctors to station themselves in the three dining rooms with whatever supplies were necessary to treat the sick or injured. The chief steward was to have hot coffee ready for the crew, as well as soup, drinks, and blankets for the rescued. Each passageway on the ship would be manned by a steward whose job was to calm the *Carpathia*'s passengers as they awoke and keep them off the deck. To bring survivors on board, lines, chair slings, and ladders were readied, along with ashbags for hoisting up the children. The captain even thought to have oil ready in case the water was rough at the rescue site — the oil would be poured down the lavatories to calm the water around the ship.

Rostron had no idea what he would find when he reached the *Titanic*. The *Carpathia* was still over forty miles from the distress position, and the last message he'd received had sounded grim. "Engine room getting flooded." Was it in his power to save the thousands of lives in need of rescue? The worst possibility could not be considered.

Meanwhile, in the place where the *Titanic* had sunk, a spine-chilling chorus drifted across the water — a mixture of cries, screams, and shouts. For those sitting or standing in the lifeboats, shivering in the cold, it was the most nightmarish sound imaginable. Few, however, were moved to help the hundreds dying in the water. Most feared they would be swamped by rowing into such a throng.

In lifeboat No. 1, Leading Fireman Charles Hendrickson proposed going back, but Lady Duff Gordon muttered something about swamping, while several of the male passengers agreed it would be dangerous. Hendrickson thought one of them was her husband, but Fireman James Taylor, sitting beside Sir Cosmo, testified

Captain Arthur Rostron (left) and his ship, the Cunard liner Carpathia (right).

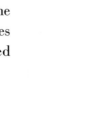

afterward that he did not respond. At Henry Stengel's suggestion they instead rowed for the light still visible in the distance. The boat contained only twelve people. There was room for over two dozen more.

Some voices did urge an attempt at rescue. In lifeboat No. 8 the Countess of Rothes, her cousin Gladys Cherry, Seaman Thomas Jones and an American woman wanted to return for

Only boat No. 4, with Quartermaster Perkis in charge, returned to the scene. The women on board soon pulled five crewmen from the water. Among them was Storekeeper Frank Prentice, who had stayed in the water with his unconscious friend, Cyril Ricks, until he died. Prentice, sluggish from being nearly frozen, had in his pocket a bottle of brandy he had salvaged from a storeroom. When Perkis saw the bottle, he

(Left) The role played by the ladies in the lifeboats as captured by a 1912 magazine artist. In boat No. 8, Seaman Jones handed over the tiller to the Countess of Rothes (below) and later gave her the number "8" from the lifeboat mounted on a plaque, in gratitude for her assistance that night.

the swimmers, but they were overruled by the majority. "Ladies," Jones told the group, "if any of us are saved, remember I wanted to go back. I would rather drown with them than leave them."

In boat No. 6, which had earlier ignored Captain Smith's order to return to the sinking ship, most of the passengers now argued in favor of returning, but Quartermaster Hichens countered by graphically describing how the desperate drowning people would capsize their boat. It was useless to go back for a lot of "stiffs," he maintained.

"It is no use arguing with that man at all," Major Peuchen told the ladies. "It is best not to discuss matters with him."

grabbed it and tossed it away. Martha Stephenson of Haverford, Pennsylvania, was convinced the bottle was thrown overboard because Prentice was drunk. Prentice, however, assumed it had been taken away from him because Perkis feared the liquor might cause some of the women to become hysterical.

The water was so lethally cold that of the five men boat No. 4 rescued from the water in the half hour after the ship went down, only Steward Andrew Cunningham remained conscious. Later, when Trimmer Thomas Dillon awoke, he found two crewmen lying on top of him, dead.

Of the twenty boats now scattered across the surface, a few were close enough for those in the

In this newspaper illustration, Captain Smith reaches overturned collapsible B and gallantly hands over a baby he has rescued before vanishing. Although some claim Smith did appear at boat B, there is no evidence that he saved an infant.

water to reach them. The closest of all were collapsible A and the overturned collapsible B. Colonel Gracie had surfaced just after the sinking. He had unsuccessfully attempted to straddle a crate, finally spied collapsible B, which was surrounded by dozens of swimmers, and swam over. When no one attempted to help him on board, he grabbed the arm of a crewman and pulled himself on.

After thirty men had climbed onto the overturned boat, including Second Officer Lightoller, they tried to paddle away from the remaining swimmers using a loose board. "Look out, you will swamp us," someone told A. H. Barkworth, one of the last to climb on. Colonel Gracie turned

his back to the crowd in the water, not wanting to be called upon to refuse anyone access.

"Hold on to what you have, old boy. One more of you aboard would sink us all," one of the crewmen called to a man in the water. In a powerful voice the swimmer called back, "All right, boys. Good luck and God bless you." Several men would later claim to have recognized the swimmer as Captain Smith. He swam away for a short distance before becoming still.

By this time collapsible B was crowded with men standing, sitting or kneeling in all conceivable positions, afraid to move for fear of losing their grip on the boat's hull. Young Jack Thayer, whose life until now had been a sheltered one of wealth and prestige, found his companions to be a "grimy, wiry, disheveled, hard looking lot." Colonel Gracie found some of their expressions extremely uncouth, and thinking he might be the only passenger among them decided to keep quiet. If there was any trouble keeping the raft afloat, he didn't want to be the first to go.

Both Thayer's and Gracie's first impressions were altered when a voice suggested, "Don't the rest of you think we ought to pray?" The speaker took a quick poll and found the group to be comprised of Roman Catholics, Presbyterians, and Episcopalians. Soon all were united in reciting the Lord's Prayer.

The people standing in collapsible A — still upright but with its canvas sides down — were knee-deep in water. When Olaus Abelseth reached the boat he was close to exhaustion. When he'd surfaced after the sinking he first had to extricate himself from a tangle of rope, then fight off two swimmers who tried to use him as a lifebuoy. His two relatives Peter and Sigurd were gone, apparently drowned. It was a miracle he'd made it this far, but the people standing and kneeling in collapsible A were far from welcoming. Someone muttered, "Don't capsize the boat," so Abelseth clung to the side for a few minutes before deciding that it was safe to climb on. Among those already aboard was Rhoda Abbott of Providence, Rhode Island, who had jumped from the ship with her two teenage sons. The boys were nowhere to be seen.

"Well, let's try to organize," someone in the bow announced. The occupants tried counting off to see how many there were, but some of the non-English-speakers didn't understand what was being done, and when they had finished the results were soon forgotten. Someone thought of erecting the canvas sides and bailing out the swamped boat. One man tried to borrow another's hat to use for bailing, but the owner, though soaked from head to toe like his com-

panions, refused, insisting he would "catch cold in the night air." After struggling with the sides it was discovered that the supports were broken and the canvas torn. "Does anyone know if our wireless messages were answered?" one man asked. No one did. Finally the occupants of collapsible A prayed as a group, still standing as their boat sank deeper in the freezing water.

As those in the boats listened, the sounds of the people struggling in the ocean gradually died away until, around 3:00 A.M., forty minutes after the *Titanic* had sunk, they ceased. Now the twenty lifeboats drifted alone in the darkness of the North Atlantic.

In lifeboat No. 1, friction had developed as Henry Stengel attempted to take charge. He was continually calling "Boat ahoy" into the darkness and suggesting which way they ought to row. Sir Cosmo Duff Gordon finally asked him to be quiet. They had been pulling around, hailing other boats and going nowhere. Lady Duff Gordon was seasick, and several of the crewmen were lying on the floor of the boat to avoid the cold air. Around 3:00 A.M. Lucile turned to her secretary, Laura Francatelli, and remarked, "There is your beautiful nightdress, gone."

"Never mind about your nightdress, madam, as long as you have got your life," Fireman Robert Pusey told her. Turning to her husband he remarked, "I suppose you have lost everything?"

"Of course," Sir Cosmo replied.

"But you can get some more?" Pusey asked.

"Yes," he acknowledged.

"Well, we have lost all our kit and the company won't give us any more," Pusey explained, "and what is more our pay stops from tonight. All they will do is send us back to London."

"You fellows need not worry about that," Sir Cosmo told him. "I will give you a fiver each to start a new kit."

By now Fifth Officer Lowe, in lifeboat No. 14,

Great controversy surrounded the behavior of Sir Cosmo and Lady Duff Gordon in lifeboat No. 1. His offer of £5 to each crewman on board was seen by many as an attempt to bribe the men into not returning to save others. Fireman George Hendrickson (above) later testified that he had wanted to row back to pick up survivors, but was overruled. The draft (below) was given to Seaman E.J. Horswell (below right).

The pitifully tiny contingent that escaped in lifeboat No. 1 posed on board the Carpathia *for a group photograph.*

had managed to round up a number of the other boats. He soon located Nos. 10, 12, and collapsible D and, upon finding there was no officer in any of them, took command. Ordering them to keep together, he explained, "If there is a passing steamer they will see a large object like that on the water quicker than they would a small one."

Boat No. 4 soon joined the tiny flotilla, and although not one of the five was by any means empty, Lowe reasoned he could safely distribute his passengers among the others and return for swimmers. Like those in the other boats, he feared a dense throng of swimmers would swamp a lifeboat, so he waited until the cries and screams had subsided and then called out to the other boats, "Are there any seamen there?"

"Yes, sir," came a reply.

"All right. You will have to distribute these passengers among these boats," Lowe ordered. "Tie them all together and come into my boat to go over into the wreckage and pick up anyone that is alive there."

As Lowe began hustling his passengers into the other lifeboats, a shawled figure caught his

attention; it seemed in too much of a hurry. He ripped the shawl off and found himself staring into the face of a man. Without a word he heaved the stowaway into the empty bow of an adjacent boat and continued until No. 14 was sufficiently empty to make a rescue attempt.

Lowe then ordered the other boats to lay on their oars, and he had his small crew pull back toward the wreck. The men could hardly row, the water was so thick with corpses. Seaman Frank Evans couldn't even bring himself to look over the side of the boat for fear he would break down. Seaman Edward Buley turned over several men's bodies, apparently frozen to death.

It was over an hour since the ship had gone down, and Lowe found only three swimmers still living. William F. Hoyt, a lace importer from New York, was a large man, and so heavy it took all the men to drag him into the boat. He was bleeding from his nose and mouth, and the men propped him up, removed his collar, and loosened his shirt. He would die within a few hours. The others, Steward Jack Stewart and a Chinese passenger, were in somewhat better shape.

As the men continued their grisly search, they suddenly heard a voice calling for help, and in the darkness they could make out a figure kneeling on a piece of wreckage. Bath Attendant Harold Phillimore had jumped from the boat deck as the ship had started to plunge and eventually crawled aboard a piece of paneling along with another man. His companion had grown steadily weaker until, muttering "What a night," he had rolled off.

Although they were only a short distance away, it took the men of boat No. 14 half an hour to push slowly through the bodies to reach Phillimore. As they drew near, Steward Alfred Pugh extended an oar to Phillimore, but he was too numb to grasp it. Finally they drew close enough for Pugh to grab the shoulder strap of Phillimore's lifebelt and pull him into the boat.

The passengers waiting in the other lifeboats were strongly affected by the cold air. The lifebelts protected torsos, but limbs and faces grew numb. In collapsible D Winnie Troutt, still holding the small baby she had saved, decided this was the coldest night she had ever experienced and wondered if her nose would ever thaw out.

Occasionally boats attempted to signal one another. In boat No. 15 the men wrapped rags, handkerchiefs, and pieces of flannel around the end of a boathook to make a torch, but each time it was lit it burned only briefly, and they finally gave up. In boat No. 2 Fourth Officer Boxhall was better prepared. He had brought some green flares from the *Titanic*'s wheelhouse. He lit one

occasionally, and the first few fooled the other lifeboats into thinking a ship was approaching.

As the night wore on, the conversation in the boats returned time and again to the chances of rescue. "This is no joke," a crewman told the occupants of No. 13. "We may knock about here days before we are picked up, if at all." One of the ship's stokers was more optimistic. "The sea will be covered with ships tomorrow afternoon," he explained. "They will race up from all over the sea to find us." In lifeboat No. 9 Kate Buss, Marion Wright, and several others spoke of Rev. and Mrs. Carter, hoping and praying the two had been saved. That very morning Lilian Carter had told Marion Wright of the class of little

(Above) On the Verge of the Ice Floe, *an artist's impression of the beautiful dawn that greeted the cold and weary survivors. Overturned collapsible B (left) provided refuge for twenty-eight people. Here, crewmen from a ship later sent to the disaster site attempt to salvage it.*

children back in Whitechapel that would so greatly miss her.

In boat No. 5 Karl Behr was rubbing his fiancée's wet stocking feet when someone nudged him. He stood upright to find a man holding a nickel-plated revolver. "Should the worse come to the worst," the stranger whispered, "you can use this revolver for your wife, after my wife and I have finished with it." He spoke so calmly that Behr politely thanked him for his offer.

Relations between the commander of boat No. 6 and his passengers remained poisonous. Quartermaster Hichens continued to criticize those at the oars. "Here, you fellow on the starboard side," he called to Lookout Frederick Fleet, "your oar is not being put in the water at the right angle." The women tried to taunt him into taking an oar, but with no success. When the light toward which they had been pulling gradually disappeared, Hichens began moaning that they were likely to drift for days. They were hundreds of miles from land with no food, water, or protection of any kind. Seeing a flask held by one of the ladies, he requested a drink and one of her wraps. She refused him the liquor, but passed him an extra blanket which he quickly wrapped about himself.

Eventually boat No. 16 drew close to boat No. 6, and the two were lashed together. Hichens ordered them to drift, but the two hulls knocked against one another so badly that at Major Peuchen's suggestion life preservers were put between them. The occupants then settled back to wait for morning.

Aboard overturned collapsible B one talkative crew member recognized Second Officer Lightoller. "We will all obey what the officer orders," he called out. The presence of an officer gave the men some encouragement, and Lightoller soon organized them in calling for help. "Now, boys, all together," he instructed, and the men would shout in unison, "Boat ahoy! Boat ahoy!"

After several tries, when no response was forthcoming, he had them stop to conserve their strength.

When Lightoller discovered that Wireless Operator Harold Bride was also aboard the collapsible, he asked what ships were on their way. Bride responded with the *Baltic*, *Olympic*, and *Carpathia*. Soon the men's eyes scanned the darkness for steamer lights. Their hopes were often raised by what they thought were ships, but which turned out to be merely a light in another lifeboat.

It seemed the night would never end. Eventually two of the men on B died, one falling back into the water. But after swimming amongst drowning people and listening to hundreds more dying, A. H. Barkworth was unmoved by the sight. "You lose your horror of the dead," he would comment afterward.

Swamped collapsible A lost even more people to the cold. The boat had sunk to the point that its occupants were nearly waist-deep in water, and the icy ocean was quickly robbing them of any body heat. A man behind Norris Williams asked if he could rest his arm on Williams' shoulder, as he felt so cold and tired. As time passed, however, his grip gradually loosened until he fell into the water, dead. Several others fell overboard as well, and two who died were thrown over to try to make the boat rise out of the water a little more. A man sitting behind Olaus Abelseth complained of cramps and, hunching over, wrapped his arms around the young Norwegian. After he died, Abelseth had to pry his arms loose.

In his own efforts to stay warm, Abelseth tried to keep moving, swinging his arms back and forth. Norris Williams temporarily forgot the cold by becoming preoccupied with a man wearing a derby with a dent in one side. He tried to persuade the man to push the dent out, but the stranger didn't seem to understand, even after attempts to explain in German, Italian, French, and with gestures and sign language. In exasperation Williams reached for the derby to fix it himself, but the owner resisted, apparently thinking he wanted to take it.

While the lifeboats drifted on the still, calm ocean, the *Carpathia* continued to race recklessly through the night, dodging icebergs as she came. Shortly after 2:30 a lookout spotted a green light far off the port bow. "There's his light!" Rostron exclaimed. "He must still be afloat." His optimism proved unfounded; the light disappeared. Another half hour passed, and there was no sign of the ship. Yet Rostron barreled on through a sea littered with bergs, firing rockets every fifteen minutes. Now, just after 3:30 A.M., he had all but given up hope. They were close to the *Titanic*'s distress position and had seen no trace of the great liner. Still, he pressed on.

More than an hour had passed since the *Titanic*'s sinking, and the morale in the boats was ebbing fast when someone in boat No. 13 pointed out a faint, faraway glow to the southeast. There came a slight boom, and then the light died. Fred Barrett, who had been lying at the stern, suddenly sat up and cried, "That was a cannon!" In boat No. 6, Margaret Martin was pulling on an oar when she, too, saw the light and commented, "There is a flash of lightning." Quartermaster Hichens disagreed. "It is a falling star," he replied.

First one masthead light appeared on the horizon, then another, and soon a green running light. Now there was no question that a big steamer was coming hard, firing rockets as she came. Then the ship gradually slowed. As she coasted toward boat No. 2 Fourth Officer Boxhall lit one last green flare. "Shut down your engines and take us aboard," he cried up to the Cunarder's bridge. "I have only one sailor."

"All right," a voice called back. It belonged to Captain Rostron.

"The *Titanic* has gone down with everyone on board!" Mrs. Mahala Douglas screamed from beside the tiller. Boxhall immediately followed with "Shut up!" and Mrs. Douglas fell silent. The *Carpathia* was soon right alongside the tiny boat, and a rope ladder was extended down to the occupants. Boxhall assisted each passenger by placing a rope under their arms before he or she began to climb.

When everyone from boat No. 2 had been taken aboard, Boxhall left the boat and was escorted by Second Officer Bisset to the bridge. There, Rostron asked the *Titanic*'s fourth officer if his ship had gone down. The answer was obvious, yet he had to make certain.

"Yes," Boxhall replied solemnly. "She went down at about 2:30." He quickly began detailing what had happened until Rostron interrupted, "Were many people left on board when she sank?"

"Hundreds and hundreds! Perhaps a thousand! Perhaps more!" Boxhall burst out emotionally. "My God, sir, they've gone down with her. They couldn't live in this icy cold water."

"Thank you, mister," Rostron finally said. "Go below and get some coffee, and try to get warm."

I T WAS NOW PAST 4:00 A.M., AND AS THE lifeboats began rowing toward the lights of the *Carpathia*, there appeared in the east the faint golden glow of dawn. The stars gradually dimmed, and the outline of the ship was revealed, its single funnel spewing black smoke into the lightening sky. To Henry Sleeper Harper in boat No. 3, she looked tiny compared to the mammoth liner they had been watching only a few hours before, but she was at that moment a beautiful and welcome sight.

With the dawn there appeared what many took to be several sailing ships on the water. However, as the light grew, it became obvious these weren't ships at all, but icebergs, the sunlight turning them pink, mauve, blue, and white.

Among the passengers on the Carpathia *was a successful American artist by the name of Colin Campbell Cooper. (Right) One of the gouache paintings he made of the rescue.*

Winnie Troutt, in collapsible D, was struck by the irony that such beauty could also have been the cause of such horror. In boat No. 14 fifteen-year-old Edith Brown of Johannesburg found the scene so tranquil and lovely that she could hardly believe a ship such as the *Titanic* had ever been there at all.

Watching the *Carpathia* was agony to the men clinging to overturned collapsible B. With morning had come a slight swell, and the air was gradually leaking out from under their boat, causing it to sink lower and lower until the water washed over the hull. Charles Lightoller had the men stand in two columns and instructed them to lean left or right as needed to keep the boat on an even keel. Harold Bride, however, was unable to join them. Someone had been sitting on his legs to the point where he could not stand.

Soon after the men got to their feet, Chief Baker Charles Joughin, who had stepped blithely off the stern as the *Titanic* sank, came swimming up to the boat. Miraculously, he had been paddling around in the water for two hours, oblivious to the cold. Undoubtedly he owed his survival to the considerable amount of alcohol he had consumed before the sinking, which had functioned as an effective antifreeze.

When Joughin tried to climb aboard the collapsible, however, someone pushed him back into the water. Without a word he swam around to the other side of the boat where he recognized Assistant Cook John Maynard. Joughin grabbed the hand Maynard extended and hung on, floating with his lifebelt and making no further effort to climb from the water.

Under the brightening sky the men on collapsible B discovered boats Nos. 10, 12, 4, and collapsible D still lashed together on the opposite side of them from the *Carpathia*. Stiff with the cold, Lightoller managed to fish into his pocket, produce a whistle, and blow. "Come over and take us off!" he shouted.

In boat No. 12 Seaman Frederick Clench heard the whistle and looked off in the distance. It appeared to him as if some men were standing on one of the ship's funnels. "Aye, aye," he called back. "I am coming over." The four boats separated, and Nos. 12 and 4 slowly began to pull toward the overturned lifeboat.

Those remaining on swamped collapsible A had begun counting to three and then screaming, but without attracting the attention of the *Carpathia*. With the daylight Olaus Abelseth discovered that one of the boat's occupants was a New Jersey gentleman with whom he had shared a compartment on the boat train. The man was lying semiconscious in the boat, and Abelseth raised him up by one shoulder.

"We can see a ship now," Abelseth told him. "Brace up."

"Who are you?" the man responded blankly. "Let me be. Who are you?"

Abelseth continued to hold the man until he grew too tired. Finally he propped him up with a board. Within half an hour the man had died.

The second lifeboat to reach the *Carpathia* was boat No. 1. With only a dozen occupants, including Sir Cosmo and Lady Duff Gordon as well as seven crewmen who were pulling at the oars, it quickly outdistanced the other boats.

Gradually, more heavily laden boats approached. In boat No. 13 the occupants joined together in a verse of "Pull for the Shore, Sailor." Their voices trailed off, and the song was followed with a cheer, which drew more enthusiasm.

Boats Nos. 6 and 16 were still tied together and, as Quartermaster Hichens had ordered, still drifting. When someone asked Hichens if the ship in the distance would come to rescue them, he replied, "No, she is not going to pick us up. She is to pick up bodies."

Neither Molly Brown, Helen Candee, a noted authoress, nor the other women were about to allow the perverse quartermaster to prevent them

COLIN CAMPBELL COOPER

An impressionist who had been influenced by the work of Claude Monet and Childe Hassam, Colin Campbell Cooper was best known for his paintings of streetscapes and architectural subjects. He and his wife Emma, also an artist, gave up their stateroom on the Carpathia *to three women survivors, among them René*

Harris, the wife of well-known theatrical producer Henry B. Harris, who had gone down with the Titanic. *Campbell completed his two scenes of the rescue after the* Carpathia *resumed her voyage to the Mediterranean. Here he poses on board ship with his finished works.*

The second of the two rescue paintings by Colin Campbell Cooper.

from being rescued. One man in boat No. 16 looked so cold, dressed only in pajamas with his teeth chattering, that Mrs. Brown told him to start rowing to keep his blood circulating. Hichens protested, but the women joined the Colorado millionairess in demanding they be allowed to row to keep warm. From boat No. 6 they borrowed a stoker, still grimy with coal dust, who took an oar on the starboard side. Molly Brown picked up a large sable stole she had dropped in the bottom of the boat and wrapped it around

his legs, tying the tails around his ankles. She then ordered the man in pajamas to cut the two boats apart.

Hichens was fast losing what little remained of his command. He howled in protest and moved to prevent the two boats from being cut loose, but Molly Brown told him she would throw him overboard if he interfered. Hichens was visibly frightened by her threat, and as the boats cast apart and the women began rowing, he sank back under his blanket at the tiller and began swearing

153

and shouting insults at the Denver woman.

"I say," the stoker called out incredulously. "Don't you know you are talking to a lady?"

"I know whom I am speaking to and I am commanding this boat!" Hichens shouted back. His words fell on deaf ears. The woman who would become known as "The Unsinkable Molly Brown" was now in charge, and the boat slowly rowed to the *Carpathia*.

One way or another, as the sun rose higher in the sky, the lifeboats made their way to the *Carpathia*. Boat No. 14 hoisted a sail and towed collapsible D along. On their way they encountered collapsible A, and soon Fifth Officer Lowe had its few remaining passengers in his boat. Boats Nos. 12 and 4 detoured to take on Lightoller and the other men from collapsible B. Charles Joughin, still in the water, was the first to board boat No. 12. He simply swam over and was quickly pulled in. Lightoller, correct and punctilious to the end, was the last to step to safety. The more crowded the boat, the longer it took to row toward the ladders that hung from the *Carpathia*'s side, and boat No. 12, with Lightoller in charge, was so crowded that it could only move at a snail's pace through the water.

The decks of the *Carpathia* grew increasingly crowded with her just-wakened passengers and the swelling number of *Titanic* survivors. Captain Rostron was impressed with the orderly way in which the rescued came on board. There was no hurry, no noise. Seeing how many lifeboats were only partly filled and noting how many passengers were not well clothed, he imagined how hurriedly they must have vacated the *Titanic*, and felt sympathy for the fear they must have felt that the ship would go down before they could get away.

Most of the survivors needed help making it up the ladders. Some were in a very bad way indeed. Rescued from collapsible A, Fireman John Thompson's jaw was locked shut from the

cold, and when he went to climb the ladder he discovered that he had apparently broken his arm when the ship foundered. Coming from the same boat was Steward Edward Brown, whose feet were swollen to the point where they had burst open his boots. Before anyone attempted to ascend, a rope was slung under their arms or tied around their waists, and they were hoisted more than they climbed.

Even this prospect was too much for some. Kate Buss, arriving in boat No.9, was so fearful of heights that she held back, continually finding an excuse not to leave the lifeboat. When another woman slipped and dangled by the safety rope, her terror deepened. Only when Kate was the only woman left in the boat did she force herself to ascend. As she stepped onto the deck of the *Carpathia* she heard a voice cry out, "Bring out the swings! No more ladders!" at which point she began laughing hysterically and buried her face in the blanket wrapped around her.

In boat No. 13, Ruth Becker's hands were so cold that she couldn't grip the ropes; she simply let the crewmen lift her on board — ever fearful she would slip out — where she was immediately offered coffee and brandy. She declined, having never tasted either.

In all, the rescue took more than four hours. One of the last boats to arrive was collapsible C, into which Bruce Ismay had stepped just as it left the *Titanic*. Once on board Ismay stood with his back to a bulkhead, speaking to no one. The ship's surgeon, Dr. Frank McGhee, approached and asked, "Will you not go into the saloon and get some soup, or something to drink?"

"No, I really do not want anything at all," Ismay replied.

"Do go and get something," the doctor urged, realizing how distraught the man before him was.

"No. If you'll leave me alone, I will be very much happier here," Ismay explained, then added, "If you will get me in some room where

(Above) Lifeboat No. 14, under the command of Fifth Officer Lowe, towed collapsible D to the Carpathia.

*(Above) Collapsible D approaches, overloaded and awash with icy water. Her passengers include René Harris and the Navratil boys.
(Below) Boat No. 6, with Molly Brown and Major Peuchen on board, comes into view.
(Right) Quartermaster Hichens stands in the stern as it approaches the* Carpathia.

I can be quiet, I wish you would."

"Please go in the saloon and get something hot," McGhee persisted.

"I would rather not," Ismay replied. Finally the doctor gave up and took Ismay to his own quarters, where he remained until the ship arrived in New York.

Finally there remained only boat No. 12 creeping slowly toward the *Carpathia* with Second Officer Lightoller in command. He had moved a number of people aft to keep the bow up, but the boat was so crowded that the gunwales were only inches above the sea, and the water was getting rougher. Lightoller counted seventy-five people aboard, not including the children and perhaps some adults whom he couldn't see. Seaman Frederick Clench was afraid Harold Bride was going to "croak" before they could be rescued, he was in such a bad way.

Because of the lifeboats crowded along its side, Captain Rostron could not move the *Carpathia* closer to boat No. 12. If there was any shortcoming in his performance that morning, it was that he did not dispatch several boats to meet the lifeboat. As No. 12 neared the ship, one wave, then another, broke over its bow. There seemed a real possibility it would founder, but it rode the third and was soon in the shelter of the *Carpathia*. Colonel Gracie dashed up the ladder leading up the side of the ship. He was nearly tempted to kiss the deck, so grateful was he to be alive.

Even after the last survivor had safely climbed on board, a crowd still clung to the rail of the *Carpathia*, scanning the sea for further signs of life. Most were wives who had parted from their husbands on board the *Titanic* and now hoped against hope to see those loved ones again. They

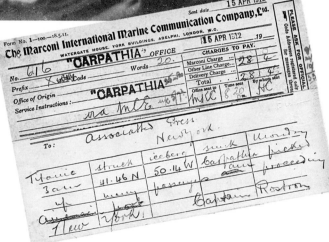

Once the passengers and lifeboats (top) were safely on board, Captain Rostron sent a terse telegram (above) to the Associated Press. This was the first firm news the world received of the Titanic's fate.

(Above) As a lone crewman pokes his head out to watch, some of the last passengers prepare to board the Carpathia.
(Below and above right) Stunned survivors huddle together aboard the Carpathia, *comforting the bereaved and trying to come to terms with the enormity of the tragedy. The photograph below shows newlywed couple Mr. and Mrs. George Harder speaking with Mrs. Beckwith.*

waited in vain. When the ship's engines started, Ruth Becker watched the sad scene as the women were led away from the rail and taken inside. They were now widows.

As the *Carpathia* briefly cruised the area, two services were held. One was a short prayer of thanksgiving for the 705 who had been rescued, and the other a funeral service for the more than 1,500 people who had perished. While many of the passengers were thus distracted, Captain Rostron looked for any last survivors. The remnants of the *Titanic* had apparently drifted away, for he found very little — mostly loose cork that had been used as insulation between bulkheads. He saw only one body.

At 8:50 A.M. the *Carpathia* sailed away, leaving the Leyland liner *Californian*, which had arrived on the scene nearly an hour earlier, to continue the search. Almost immediately Rostron found his way blocked by a huge ice field stretching as far as he could see. He began steaming parallel to it, from time to time passing isolated bergs. This was the field described by the *Mesaba's* ice message on Sunday night — the message that failed to reach the *Titanic's* bridge.

WHILE CAPTAIN ROSTRON PONDERED what to do with the survivors, the news of the disaster was spreading across the globe. White Star vice-president Phillip A. S. Franklin in New York had been awakened at 1:40 A.M. by a telephone call from a reporter who told him the *Titanic* had radioed for assistance and was sinking. When Franklin asked where he had heard such surprising news, the man replied it was from the steamer *Virginian* via Montreal. As soon as Franklin hung up, he called the White

Star dock, but those on duty there knew only what reporters had told them.

Increasingly worried, Franklin contacted the Associated Press, which had no more information. When he asked if the news agency couldn't hold such an alarming story until it could be confirmed, the reply was curt. "No. It has gone out." Whether or not the *Titanic* was in trouble, Franklin clearly had a public-relations crisis on his hands. So he telephoned various White Star Line officials, asking them to meet him at the company offices on Broadway. Not wishing to alarm Captain Haddock of the *Olympic*, he sent a marconigram to the liner asking simply, "Make every effort to communicate *Titanic* and advise position and time. Reply to Ismay, New York."

Upon arriving at the company offices, Franklin and his men confronted the worst in the form of a long memorandum from the Associated Press describing the distress messages, giving the positions of the *Baltic*, *Olympic*, and *Virginian*, and stating that at 12:25 Eastern Standard Time the *Titanic*'s signals blurred and ended abruptly. Franklin mentally worked out the positions of the other ships in order to see how far assistance was from the crippled liner.

By morning newspapers carrying the story were on the street, and crowds had begun gathering outside the offices. But Franklin still had no definite word. Most newspapers continued to cling to the belief in the *Titanic*'s unsinkability, but the *New York Times* had taken the abrupt end of the distress signals to mean only one thing. The morning edition reported that the ship had gone down. Although based upon supposition, it proved to be one of the greatest journalistic scoops in history.

Florence Ismay and her younger children were still enjoying their automobile tour of Wales when the news of the collision reached them in the coastal town of Fishguard. She immediately ordered the chauffeur to drive them home to

(Above) On the morning of April 15, anxious crowds gather outside the New York offices of the White Star Line.
(Left) The day after the sinking, the New York Times *headline indicates just how incomplete the news still was.*

(Top) Outside the offices of the New York Sun, *people wait for the latest news.*
(Above) *Mrs. Benjamin Guggenheim on the steps of White Star's New York offices. As late as mid-morning, she was told there was no need to worry.*

Liverpool. Meanwhile, the Ismays' daughter Margaret, returning from her honeymoon, was met in London by an aunt who told her of the accident. The young woman was soon en route to Liverpool to join the rest of the family in awaiting news of the ship and of her father.

In Southampton, home to hundreds of the *Titanic*'s crew, the half-pay notes (which allowed the wives to collect part of their husbands' salaries without waiting for them to come home) had become payable. Many of the women gathered after cashing the notes to discuss the news reports that the *Titanic* had struck an iceberg and was sinking. A number of the women had more than one family member aboard the ship. Still, there was no firm word of the *Titanic*'s fate.

Aboard the *Carpathia*, Captain Rostron was still debating what to do with the survivors when he stopped by the doctor's cabin to see Bruce Ismay. "Don't you think, sir, you had better send a message to New York, telling them about this accident?" the captain asked.

Despite his dazed state, Ismay agreed and wrote out, "Deeply regret advise you *Titanic* sank this morning after collision iceberg, resulting serious loss life. Full particulars later. Bruce Ismay."

"Captain," Ismay asked, "do you think that is all I can tell them?"

"Yes," Rostron replied. He could see that Ismay was a broken man. His ship was gone with over 1,500 people. A voyage begun as the crowning achievement of his career had ended in a disaster unequaled in maritime history. Later, when the captain consulted him regarding what Rostron considered to be an unwise request by the *Olympic* — to transfer the survivors to her, the *Titanic*'s almost identical twin sister — Ismay's response was emphatic. The *Olympic* was to stay out of sight. Since he continued to make no effort to leave the cabin, a sign was hung on the door to prevent people looking for Dr. McGhee from

continually walking in. With no appetite for solid food, Ismay lived on soup until reaching shore.

Once Captain Rostron had decided to keep the survivors, he had to determine what to do with them. It was ridiculous to consider finishing the voyage to the Mediterranean. Halifax was closer than New York, but there was a great deal of ice on that route. After consulting Ismay once more, they decided upon New York. Rostron sent a message to the Cunard offices there expressing his intent to sail for that port unless otherwise ordered.

As the *Carpathia* steamed southward along the edge of the seemingly endless icefield, for a time escorted by several whales, many reunions were taking place between people separated during the sinking. Ruth Becker was helping to look for the lost baby of the young immigrant mother who had stood beside her in boat No. 13 when a strange woman confronted her and asked, "Are you Ruth Becker?" After the girl replied yes, the woman explained, "Your mother has been looking everywhere for you." Moments later Ruth was reunited with her mother, her sister, and brother. Later she discovered that her friend had found the missing child.

Ruth Dodge was one of only four women to find their husbands safe on the *Carpathia*. Her four-year-old son had seen his father first, but thought it would be a game to hide from him. He could not understand why his mother was angry when he finally announced, "I have seen Daddy!"

By nightfall the *Carpathia* had cleared the last of the ice and was well on her way to New York. After supper the rescued began searching for places to sleep. The *Carpathia*'s passengers had already donated clothing, and now many gave up their berths or took in people to fill spare ones. Soon mattresses and blankets filled the public rooms. Women with children were given first priority for staterooms. The lounges and dining saloons were reserved for the use of women without children. When mattresses ran short, a folded steamer rug took its place, with a second as a cover. In the lounges, sofa cushions were quickly grabbed up as pillows. One elderly woman slept on a bench while her sister was on the floor beside her, referring to it as a "lower berth in the *Carpathia* Pullman."

No room was spared. Mrs. Marie Jerwan slept on the floor of the galley, while Lawrence Beesley curled up on a stack of towels in a bathroom. He was awakened in the middle of the night by a man with a four-berth stateroom whose roommate could not be moved and

therefore could not give up the room to women. Beesley gladly accepted a spare bunk. The Beckers were assigned beds in the crew's quarters. Not surprisingly, being so far down in the ship made Ruth so nervous that she was almost unable to sleep.

Men slept in the smoking rooms, but these were so crowded that some even chose to sleep out on deck. Olaus Abelseth found some floor space, where he slept wearing the same salt-encrusted clothing in which he had been rescued from collapsible A.

At least one survivor tried to take more than his share. After dinner Alfred Nourney, the young

John A. Badenoch, a director of Macy's, sent this telegram to the Strauses' son Percy from on board the Carpathia.

THE FENWICKS' MEMENTOS

The honeymoon trip on the *Carpathia* of James and Mabel Fenwick (left) took an unexpected turn early on the morning of April 15. Mabel was awakened by a man's voice crying *"Titanic*'s going down!" She dressed hurriedly and went on deck, bringing along her camera. Her first photograph (upper left) shows the sea flecked with drift ice. Then a sail appears (lower left), lifeboat No. 14. At around 8:30 A.M., well after the rescue had been completed, the *Californian* steams up (middle top), and near noon, they passed the liner *Birma* (middle bottom). Later Mrs. Fenwick persuaded Captain Arthur Rostron and his officers to pose for a group portrait (top right). She also captured Lawrence Beesley in his dressing gown, flanked by two other survivors (right), and third-class passengers (far right) in line for a meal.

A 573
CUNARD S.S. CO. Ltd.
R.M.S. CARPATHIA.
RECEIVED FOR
(HIRE)
DECK CHAIR.
4/- or 1 Dollar.

CUNARD LINE
Cabin Baggage
A 21
Stateroom
On S. S. *Carpathia* Sailing
Passenger's Name *Fenwick*

Arthur Peuchen's laconic cable home was never sent. Operator Thomas Cottam, although aided by Harold Bride, simply couldn't get through the mountain of messages.

man from Cologne who had been traveling as "Baron Von Drachstedt," had gone into the first-class smoking room and made a very comfortable bed out of a tall stack of blankets intended for distribution among the survivors. When a group of young women entered and saw what he had done, one grabbed the blanket just beneath him and rolled him off. "And to think such as you were saved," she scolded, the room applauding as Nourney made a hasty exit.

That night there still was no sleep for the *Carpathia's* wireless operator, Thomas Cottam, who had remained at his post once the *Titanic's* distress call was received the previous night. Even before the last lifeboat had arrived, personal messages from survivors began pouring into his office. Now he also patiently transmitted the names of the rescued to the *Olympic*, whence they would be relayed ashore.

By Tuesday morning the full impact of the tragedy began to manifest itself among the survivors. Dozens of women gathered in the dining saloons where, dressed in everything from night-clothes to evening wear, they sat and wept. Many wailed that had they known their husbands were to drown they would not have left them. When these women saw Nellie Becker in the second-class dining saloon with her three children, some would frequently ask, "How did it happen you were all saved?" Others, in an attempt to lift her spirits, jokingly accused her of saving more than her share.

Ruth Becker, not as distraught as her mother, found little to do. Being with the sobbing women was awkward, so she sat on the floor with the other children, occasionally sneaking sugar lumps from the tables. When that grew boring she would steal away and walk the decks where she often witnessed widows approaching men and asking, "How were you saved? How did you get in a boat?"

Winnie Troutt seemed to be handling the

shock quite well. She had given the baby she had saved to a crewman who promised to reunite the child with its mother. When another female survivor asked if she had lost everything, she answered affirmatively and without emotion. "Why, you poor girl, lost everything?" the woman asked incredulously. "Didn't you save your powder? I'll give you some." She wrapped some powder in a handkerchief and gave it to her. Miss Troutt graciously accepted it, struggling to keep a straight face. Another woman sought to comfort others through her belief in Christianity and salvation. "You women, why do you cry for your husbands?" she asked, confronting a group of widows. "My husband is gone, but I know he's saved." Her religion did not soothe her financial losses, however, as she suddenly cried out, "But all my jewels are *gone*! All my jewels!" Laugh and the world laughs with you, Winnie thought. Cry and you cry alone.

Norris Williams, who had seen his father killed and then stood for hours waist-deep in near freezing water on collapsible A, felt that many of his fellow survivors were exaggerating their experiences. He finally lost his temper with one woman who complained of having been in a boat with so few men that she had blistered her hands helping to row.

One unattractive scene was played repeatedly during the voyage to New York. Nurse Alice Cleaver refused to allow Sarah Daniels near little Trevor Allison, the only member of the Allison family to survive the sinking, even when he would cry out and stretch his arms toward Sarah. In contrast, each day she allowed William Faulkner, who had carried the infant into boat No. 11 for her, to visit the child. No doubt she saw the Allison baby as some sort of insurance: as long as she had him in her clutches, she was safe. As the child's savior, perhaps she could even work this to her financial advantage.

Quartermaster Robert Hichens, who also had

(Left) A newsboy hawks the startling news to bystanders outside Oceanic House on Cockspur Street near Trafalgar Square, London headquarters of the White Star Line. As word spread, the crowds increased (below).
(Above) Oceanic House as it looks today, many years after the last White Star ship has gone.

bad behavior to hide, received no sympathy from the women who had been with him in boat No. 6. At one point he was in a dining room animatedly describing to a crowd the difficulty he had suffered in maintaining discipline before they were rescued. When he saw Molly Brown and a few others from the lifeboat enter the room, however, he halted his story and hurriedly left.

The Carpathia's voyage to New York passed gloomily. Worsening the already frayed nerves of those on board was a storm that began late Tuesday night. When it struck, Karl Behr was asleep on a smoking-room table. He awoke to a loud crash, jumped from the table, and raced from the room. Thinking the Carpathia, too, had hit an iceberg, he wanted to reach his fiancée, Helen Newsom. But when he arrived on deck he was met by a blinding flash of lightning. Relieved, he returned to his makeshift bed.

A number of survivors spent the voyage recuperating from serious injuries which, apart from a few broken limbs, were mostly the result of the cold. Norris Williams' legs had been so badly frozen that a physician on board recommended amputation and offered to perform the operation himself. Williams refused and made it a point to exercise his limbs by walking every two hours, day and night. Gradually his condition improved.

The storm continued through Wednesday, adding a thick fog to the driving rain that kept almost everyone inside. The crowded public rooms, the dismal weather, and the incessant, grating bleat of the ship's foghorn got on nerves that were already on edge. Eventually it became too much for Winnie Troutt, who went into hysterics. So many fine people had gone down with the ship, including all the men at her table — even her friend Jacob Milling. It proved too much to bear. A doctor found a bed for her, which was a welcome change from the table on which she'd been sleeping, and gave her some brandy, which calmed her instantly. He advised her to get as

much fresh air as possible and she would be all right, but it would be months before she would recover.

Naturally, the recent disaster was the subject of most conversations. Second Officer Lightoller and Third Officer Pitman regularly stopped by the cabin shared by Hugh Woolner and Colonel Gracie, who was recovering from a severe blow to the head and inflamed cuts over his legs, to discuss the events of the sinking. Not surprisingly, rumors began circulating among the survivors — the captain and First Officer Murdoch had shot themselves, passengers had been shot rushing the boats, and the band had played "Nearer My God to Thee" as the ship had foundered. But the most troubling rumor was that the Titanic had received wireless warnings of ice but had not slowed down. Finally a group including Lawrence Beesley cornered one of the surviving officers, who admitted the story was true. The group turned away, unable to speak. Beesley felt an overwhelming sense of hopelessness to learn that the collision had been avoidable.

By Thursday morning, with still no sign of the storm abating, many people were at a breaking point. From the bathrooms stretched lines of people waiting to use the tubs. There seemed no escape from the dampness, but at least the food had improved as the ship approached New York and the need to conserve on supplies disappeared. The survivors' voyage through purgatory was nearing an end.

That afternoon the Carpathia picked up the foghorn of the Fire Island light, just off the south coast of Long Island. In only a few more hours the survivors would be back on dry land. Now their thoughts turned toward shore, to seeing friends and family and quietly picking up the pieces of their lives. They had no inkling of the noisy circus that would greet them, or of the controversies that were still to come.

The Titanic saga was far from over.

Thursday, April 18, 1912

A T CUNARD'S PIER 54, ON THURS-day, April 18, the crowds had been forming since late afternoon, braving the rain and cold. Now nearly 30,000 people jammed the area, which had been cordoned off by the police. Another 10,000 people filled the Battery to watch the *Carpathia* as she sailed into her berth. Behind them rose the office building of the White Star Line. Nearly the entire New York City police force was on duty that night, with hundreds of officers required to hold back the throngs. The mood was tense and expectant. Since Monday, the world had waited for the ship's arrival and with it the full story of what had happened.

At 8:00 P.M. a murmur went through the crowd as the *Carpathia* gradually appeared out of the darkness and rain. From the dozens of small craft accompanying the ship and from every building near the river, photographers' magnesium flares flashed. Unbearably slowly the little cruise ship drew closer. Strangely, she steamed past the Cunard pier and approached the White Star Line's pier instead. The reason only became obvious when she began lowering the *Titanic*'s lifeboats — all that remained of the once great liner.

Creeping back to the Cunard pier, the *Carpathia* eased into her berth. A hush fell over the friends and relatives waiting on shore. Only occasional sobbing broke the quiet. Finally the gangplank was lowered, and by nine o'clock the disembarkation had begun.

The scene inside the pier was lit by huge spotlights, directed onto the crowd so survivors could identify their relatives. The first to leave the *Carpathia* were the first-class *Titanic* passengers, filing somberly down the gangway. The relative quiet disappeared as those meeting the survivors called out names. Throughout the building people struggled to see if the faces of those leaving the *Carpathia* belonged to loved ones.

When Madeleine Astor disembarked with her maid and nurse, they were met by her stepson Vincent and quickly driven away in a waiting automobile. Karl Behr found his sisters and a brother waiting for him. They led him down the dock to where his father sat in a chair, bundled in a blanket. Behr was horrified at how feeble his father looked — the days of anxiety had taken a heavy toll on the elderly gentleman. Winnie Troutt was met by two cousins who escorted her through the dense crowd to an automobile where a third relative waited with a change of clothing. Exhausted, she was amazed at how well the rented car was navigated through the thousands of spectators blocking the streets.

The disembarkation continued, the joy constantly undercut by the enormity of the tragedy. For every mother reunited with her son, or brother with sister, there was more than one reunion that would never take place.

As more and more passengers disembarked, the excitement on the pier grew into confusion and near pandemonium. Names were shouted, cameras flashed, and the crush of the crowd became almost unbearable.

In the melée, Arthur Woolcott missed finding his fiancée, Marion Wright, who finally left with another survivor, Bessie Watt, and her daughter. Marion and Arthur were reunited the next day and married on Saturday. When one man learned that all his family members on the *Titanic* were lost, he became hysterical, thrashing the air and

(Top) Harold Bride's feet were so badly frozen that he had to be carried off the Carpathia.
(Above) Although her fiancé had come to meet her at Pier 54 when she arrived in New York on the Carpathia, *Marion Wright missed seeing him in the enormous mass of people. They were reunited the next day, and their marriage took place as planned.*

(Above) Passengers emerge from the Carpathia's *gangway to confront the waiting throng at Pier 54. Outside the Cunard pier, a huge crowd of 30,000 stood in the rain and cold (far right). (Right) Before the* Carpathia *arrived at her berth, she made a stop at White Star's pier to lower the* Titanic's *lifeboats.*

THE LIFEBOATS

What happened to the *Titanic*'s lifeboats? A degree of mystery still surrounds this question. The thirteen lifeboats left at the White Star piers (top right) were visited by workmen on April 20 (bottom right) who removed the remaining company flags and nameplates. From the supplies packed in each lifeboat, this hardtack biscuit (left) is still intact, saved by *Carpathia* passengers James and Mabel Fenwick.

The fate of the lifeboats themselves is unknown, although a photograph taken shortly after of the *Olympic* in Southampton (above), with boats in the foreground, suggests they may have been brought home by the sister ship.

(Above) Although most newspapers retouched Alice Cleaver's face to make the supposed heroine look more pleasant, the Chesterville (Ontario) Record *showed her as she actually appeared.*

(Above) Three-year-old William R. Richards wears a nightgown made from a blanket on board the Carpathia. *Although his uncle was lost, he and five other members of his family were saved.*

reeling back and forth. A member of the Salvation Army approached to comfort him, but was waved away. A Catholic priest attempted as well, but by then the man's face was a purplish red, the veins in his neck bulging. "Go away! Oh, go away!" he screamed. "I don't want to see anybody or speak to anybody for a month!"

Members of the press ruthlessly pursued every angle in search of a scoop. When William Sloper walked down the gangway, he was met not only by his father and brother, but by John Gleason, the editor of the *Hartford Times*, one of the largest newspapers in Sloper's home state of Connecticut. "Have you got a story for me?" Gleason asked anxiously as they left for the Waldorf-Astoria. Newshounds sensed a bigger catch when Alice Cleaver stepped ashore, still clutching baby Trevor Allison, the sole survivor of the wealthy Montreal family.

As the reporters mobbed around, Alice fended them off with fresh falsehoods, giving her first name as "Jane" and refusing to provide a surname. In a bizarre twist, the press simply assumed that "Jane" was in fact the "Miss K. T. Andrews" whose name followed that of "Master Allison and nurse" on the list of survivors. The public, eager for heroes, did not question Alice's story of selfless sacrifice, and her true identity remained unknown.

However, the families of Hudson and Bess Allison saw nothing heroic in Miss Cleaver's behavior. They believed the nurse had panicked when she rushed on deck with Trevor, leaving Mrs. Allison in an impossible situation. She was not the type of woman to leave the ship without first knowing with absolute certainty that her baby was safe. They held Alice Cleaver indirectly responsible for the deaths of Bess, Hudson, and their daughter, Loraine. Mrs. Allison's mother would long be haunted by the idea that it could just as easily have been Hudson Allison rather than Steward William Faulkner who stepped into

lifeboat No. 11 with Trevor in his arms.

Survivors who had no one waiting for them were not allowed to disembark unattended. Nellie Becker clutched a telegram she had received from friends who intended to meet her and her children at the pier. This acted as her landing card, and she escorted her three children down the gangway, wearing a borrowed dress so small that it was bursting at the seams and would not fasten properly. Ruth sported a forlorn cloak, under which she had tied a blanket around her waist as a skirt.

Kate Buss, who still had to journey to California to meet her fiancé, had heard a rumor that those who had no one to meet them would be taken to Ellis Island, so she simply walked off the ship and into the crowd as if she were being met. Wearing only a raincoat over her dressing gown, people eyed her curiously. A representative of one charity approached her, but she assured the woman she was being met soon. A second woman, Deaconess Mathers of St. Barnabas Mission, was not as easily convinced, and she persuaded Miss Buss to leave with her.

On the pier were many representatives of immigrant aid societies, so those steerage passengers who would otherwise have had no place to go found people eager to take them. To their surprise, most were driven away in automobiles, a new experience for many of them.

One person who did not appear at the gangway was Bruce Ismay. While the *Carpathia's* passengers continued to disembark, the White Star managing director remained closeted in Dr. McGhee's cabin, alone with his private demons. However, he knew he could not avoid the world much longer. His first visitor was Phillip Franklin, the White Star vice-president whose life had been turned upside down since Monday morning. Franklin warned his employer that trouble was brewing. Senator William Alden Smith of Michigan and Senator Francis G. Newlands of

ORPHANS OF THE *TITANIC*

Among the non-British passengers who boarded the *Titanic* at Southampton were a father and two young boys. The man gave his name as Louis Hoffman, and it was understood among the other travelers that "Mrs. Hoffman" was dead.

The truth was very different. The man's real name was Michel Navratil. A Slovakian by birth, he had emigrated to France in 1902 and become a successful tailor in the city of Nice. There he met and married Marcelle Carretto, the teenage daughter of an Italian couple. Although the boys — Edmond, aged two, and Michel, not quite four — were his real sons, his wife was far from dead. The couple had recently separated and the two boys had stayed with their father over the Easter weekend. When Marcelle arrived to take them home, the three had disappeared.

Michel had spirited his children to nearby Monte Carlo with the help of friends, after convincing them that Marcelle was both an unfit mother and an unfaithful wife. There, using the alias of Louis Hoffman, he purchased three second-class tickets to New York on the new White Star liner *Titanic*. The three then sailed for England.

On board the *Titanic*, Navratil almost never let his sons out of his sight. Once while he relaxed over a card game in the smoking room, he allowed a Swiss girl, Bertha Lehmann,

Lolo and Momon, the Titanic *"orphans" (top), stayed at the New York home of Margaret Hays (left) until their mother, Marcelle (above right), now the widow of Michel Navratil (above left), arrived from France.*

who spoke French but no English, to babysit them for a few hours.

Michel may have had second thoughts after the *Titanic* sailed. While on board, he wrote a letter to his mother in Hungary, asking if his sister and her husband there could care for the boys. This may have been intended as a backup plan in case he could not remain in America.

On the night of April 14, all of Michel's plans sank with the ship. Enlisting the aid of a fellow passenger, he dressed his small sons and took them to the boat deck, placing them in collapsible D, the last boat to be launched.

On board the *Carpathia*, the many toddlers and infants separated from their families were gradually reunited, all but the two little French waifs. As the ship neared New York, Miss Margaret Hays of that city, who was fluent in French, volunteered to take charge of them until their family could be located.

In the days that followed the *Carpathia*'s arrival, newspapers across the globe carried the heartrending story of these two orphaned children. Back in Nice, Marcelle Navratil read the stories and recognized the boys as her own. The White Star Line immediately arranged her passage to New York and, on May 16, she was reunited with her young sons. Two days later, the three boarded the *Oceanic* for their return voyage to France.

It turned out that Marcelle's late husband had left her a poignant last message. Before placing young Michel in the lifeboat, he had held him close and spoken words the boy would never forget: "My child, when your mother comes for you, as she surely will, tell her that I loved her dearly and still do. Tell her that I expected her to follow us, so that we might all live happily together in the peace and freedom of the New World."

Nevada were on the pier with a subpoena requiring Ismay to testify at a formal inquiry into the disaster. Only a few minutes into the conversation, the two senators arrived and served their summons. Any hope Ismay had held of escaping quietly back across the Atlantic was now gone.

Gradually the number of survivors leaving the *Carpathia* dwindled and the crowd on the pier thinned. Among those remaining, eager looks of anxious anticipation turned to sorrow, hopelessness, and despair. The last reporters who raced from the scene with their copy were followed by sobbing men and women. By midnight the pier was empty and only the *Titanic*'s crew and a handful of passengers remained on board the silent steamer. Soon they, too, would be gone.

Fearing that many key witnesses would quickly disperse, Senator Smith wasted no time getting his inquiry underway. At ten-thirty the next morning, at the Waldorf-Astoria, he opened his investigation. He argued that an American inquiry was necessary because so many of the victims were American, but his ulterior motive was to spur the enactment of updated maritime legislation, which was as badly needed in the United States as in England.

From the start, Smith was the driving force behind the hearings, and he ran them as virtually a one-man show. Senator Newlands was the only other investigator present at the opening of the inquiry, although they would eventually be assisted by such colleagues as Senator George Perkins of California, Senator Jonathan Bourne

of Oregon, Senator Theodore Burton of Ohio, Senator F. M. Simmons of North Carolina, and Senator Duncan Fletcher of Florida. Smith personally interrogated all the key witnesses despite his gaping ignorance of matters pertaining to ships and navigation. There were countless questions to be answered, but he returned again and again to several key ones: Was the ship sufficiently equipped with lifesaving devices and were they adequately inspected? Was the ship's

(Above) Bruce Ismay waits and ponders his coming testimony before the U.S. Senate Inquiry.

route a hazardous one? Did the crew behave properly? Was the *Titanic* going too fast?

The first witness called that morning was Bruce Ismay. Smith wanted Ismay's testimony while it was still fresh in his mind. In addition to the two senators were two White Star attorneys as well as Emerson Parvin, secretary of International Mercantile Marine, Guglielmo Marconi who had been called to testify, and a few spectators and reporters. The White Star managing director appeared still worn and in shock from the disaster. His voice was barely above a whisper.

Ismay began by expressing his grief at the terrible disaster, and he offered his full support of the inquiry. His testimony was guarded and cautious. He tempered phrases with "I presume" and "I believe," and at other times claimed not to remember facts at all. Smith questioned him regarding the revolutions achieved by the engines, the type of collision and other facts that Ismay could not have known unless he had been in communication with the captain or the officers. Overall, he maintained that he was no different from any other passenger on board the *Titanic* for her maiden voyage.

The other star witnesses were Second Officer Charles Lightoller and Harold Bride, the only surviving wireless operator. Both men gave dramatic testimony about their experiences in swimming from the ship to collapsible B. Lightoller came across as a dedicated officer, and he made it plain that he did not leave the ship; the ship left him. He steadfastly refused to criticize his superior officers or the White Star Line, a stance he would maintain at the subsequent British inquiry.

For weeks the public eagerly read in the newspapers the testimony of the many witnesses Smith called. He questioned a far greater range of passengers than did the subsequent British inquiry, and it is to this fact that we owe our knowledge of many of the details of the tragedy. Their candor brought to light a number of incidents that might otherwise have been overlooked by crew. Colonel Gracie specified that on the *Carpathia*, Lightoller had admitted to firing his gun to restore order at collapsible D. Mrs. Eloise Smith and Major Peuchen described the poor behavior of Quartermaster Hichens in boat No. 6, while Mrs. Ella White could not criticize enough the incompetence of the crew in No. 8 under the command of Thomas Jones. George Harder told of the difficulty the crew had in closing some of the watertight doors near his stateroom. The

American inquiry provided the only detailed accounts recorded by a number of passengers.

Of all the information that came to light, some of the most interesting involved the Leyland Line's steamer *Californian*, which had stopped near the ice field toward which the *Titanic* was steaming. Smith interrogated the ship's captain, Stanley Lord, and two of his crewmen.

Captain Lord had seen a ship approaching shortly after 11:00 P.M. the night of April 14. He judged it to be about the size of his own vessel and asked his wireless operator what ships he had. When the operator replied only the *Titanic*, Lord assumed that this approaching steamer did not have a wireless since it appeared far too small to be the great White Star liner, over forty thousand tons larger than his own ship.

At 11:30 the *Californian*'s third officer, Charles Groves, unaware that Captain Lord had already seen this steamer, reported it to him in the chartroom. Groves was under the impression the ship was a passenger steamer due to the presence of deck lights. Lord instructed him to attempt to reach the vessel by morse lamp. When Groves tried to do so at 11:40, not quite 11:25 by the *Titanic*'s clocks, the unidentified ship suddenly seemed to extinguish its deck lights. At one point he thought the ship was morsing back, but when he looked through his binoculars he concluded it was only the masthead light flickering.

At 12:15 A.M., just prior to midnight on the *Titanic*, Groves stopped by the *Californian*'s

(Below left) American White Star vice-president Phillip Franklin escorts Bruce Ismay to the Waldorf-Astoria for his appearance at the American inquiry.

The scene in the ballroom (above and right) at the Waldorf-Astoria as Ismay is grilled by the American senators.

wireless office himself. Operator Cyril Evans, who had gone off duty, explained that the only ship he had was the *Titanic*, but when Groves put the earphones on, he heard nothing. At that time Jack Phillips had finished his Cape Race traffic, and had not yet begun to send the CQD.

After Groves' watch had ended, Second Officer Herbert Stone had Apprentice James Gibson morse the strange ship in the distance. Like Groves, he thought he was getting a response, but upon inspecting with the binoculars decided it was the masthead light. Gibson commented to Stone that the ship must have been a tramp steamer burning oil lights to have them flickering like that.

At 12:40 there was a sudden flash over the mystery ship. It appeared to be a rocket, but there was no flash of a detonator on deck. It actually seemed to come from beyond the ship. Stone reported this to Captain Lord, who was now lying down in the chartroom and who asked if they appeared to be company signals. He knew they should have been close enough to hear the report made by distress rockets. He ordered Stone to try morsing the ship again and notify him once its identity was learned.

Stone got no response to the lamp, but while he was signaling three more rockets rose up, none appearing to go higher than halfway to the masthead light. By now the unidentified ship seemed to have changed her bearing and was steaming away. Apprentice Gibson once again trained his binoculars on the ship. He saw a flash that seemed to come from her deck, and a rocket rise up. To him the ship appeared to have "a big side out of the water," as if she were listing.

Stone, however, did not feel that the ship was listing, and he reasoned that the rockets could not be indicating that the ship was in distress or she would not be steaming away. After firing eight rockets, she steamed out of sight. It was after 2:00 A.M. by the *Californian*'s clocks.

HE WAS THE LOVE OF OUR HEARTS

Many poignant letters were written in the aftermath of the tragedy. Among the more moving is this simple request, with grammar and misspellings uncorrected, from the Belfast parents of crewman Herbert Jupe. "Dear Sir, I have been inform . . . that the body of my Beloved Son Herbert Jupe, which was Electrical Engineer No. 3 on the Ill Fatted Titanic has been recovered and Buried at Sea by the Cable Steamer 'Mackay-Bennett'. . . We are extremely obliged for all your kindness to my Precious Boy. He was not Married and was the Love of our Hearts and he Loved his Home. But God gave and God has taken him. Blessed be the name of the Lord. He has left an aceing (aching) Void in our Home which cannot be filled. Please send along the Watche and Handkerchief marked H.J. Yours Truly, C. Jupe. His mother is 72 last April 4th. His father is 68 Last Feb. 9th."

None of the three men who were on the bridge that evening were questioned by Senator Smith. Instead he interrogated Wireless Operator Cyril Evans, who had been asleep through almost the entire affair, except when Third Officer Groves woke him to ask what ships he had been in contact with. Smith also questioned a Donkeyman, Ernest Gill, who happened to be on deck that night and witnessed the rockets.

Smith concluded that the *Californian* had been less than nineteen miles away, perfectly able to come to the *Titanic*'s rescue in time. His findings began a controversy that continued through the British inquiry and has not been resolved to this day.

When the Senate inquiry concluded at the end of May, Senator Smith would make a number of recommendations: that all passenger ships carry lifeboats able to accommodate everyone on board; that regular lifeboat drills be held utilizing the crews assigned to them; that steamships carry searchlights; and that there be a twenty-four-hour radio watch on all vessels. Almost immediately after the American inquiry, passenger ships were fitted with sufficient lifeboats and additional wireless operators.

After three days at the Waldorf the inquiry moved on to Washington, D. C., while most of the *Titanic* survivors, except those still required to testify, went home. The crew sailed for England on the Red Star liner *Lapland*. Ismay left at the beginning of May on the *Adriatic* and was met at Queenstown by his wife and a brother. Some *Titanic* passengers made the sad journey to Halifax, Nova Scotia, to collect the bodies recovered from the Atlantic.

On Thursday, April 17, as the *Carpathia* was steaming toward New York, the White Star Line dispatched the first of several ships to look for human remains in the area of the sinking. This

White Star hired several ships from Halifax to search for and pick up bodies from the wreck. The first on the scene was the Mackay-Bennett, *which found 306 bodies, 116 of which were buried at sea. Almost every embalmer in the Maritimes was called to Halifax, and a team of them was on board to prepare*

the remaining bodies for burial.
Meanwhile the corpses were kept
on ice in the hold.
(Top left) The cable ship Mackay-
Bennett. *(Middle left) A body is*
recovered. (Bottom left) One of the
bodies is embalmed on deck.
(Above) The Mackay-Bennett's
grisly cargo covers her foredeck.

was the small cable-laying steamer *Mackay-Bennett*. Not having read any descriptions of the disaster, Captain Lardner and his men could only make educated guesses as to what had happened to the corpses that they began bringing aboard on April 21. The victims were floating upright, buoyed by lifebelts, and appeared as if they were sleeping. Watches were stopped between 2:00 and 2:20. Wreckage of all kinds was sighted,

much of it apparently from the liner's interior.

Many of the bodies brought aboard were dressed warmly. Some even had meat and biscuits in their pockets. Crew members carried matches, tobacco, and keys. One unidentified gentleman had half a dozen diamonds sewn into the lining of his coat, and the body of Colonel John Jacob Astor was accompanied by $2,500 in cash.

The *Mackay-Bennett* continued its grim work

all week, keeping only those corpses that were identifiable or in good enough condition to be embalmed. The first-class passengers were stored in coffins on deck, while the second- and third-class passengers and the crew were sewn into canvas bags and stored in the ice-filled hold. The remainder were buried at sea.

On Friday, April 25, the steamer *Minia* arrived to relieve the *Mackay-Bennett*, which left for Halifax with 190 bodies. Another 116 had been buried at sea. The *Minia* soon recovered Charles M. Hays, president of Canada's Grand Trunk Railroad, and nearly a dozen waiters and sailors. By now wind, rain, and bad weather had scattered the remaining bodies as far as 130 miles from the scene of the wreck. After a week of searching, the crew had recovered a mere seventeen, only one of which had water in his lungs. The rest had died of exposure.

Two more ships followed: the *Mont-magny*, which left Halifax on May 6, and the *Algerine*, which sailed from St. John's on May 15. After the *Algerine* recovered only one victim, the project was abandoned.

Bodies would continue to be sighted by passing steamers, and as late as June the steamer *Ilford*, en route from Galveston to Hamburg, discovered and buried at sea the badly decomposed body of First-Class Saloon Steward W. F. Cheverton.

176

(Left) Hearses and extra coffins wait on the dock as the Mackay-Bennett *is made fast. (Right) Hearses take the bodies to a curling rink set up as a temporary morgue.*

Three cemeteries in Halifax have sections for Titanic *victims. (Above) A rabbi and two workers at the Baron de Hirsch Jewish Cemetery. (Right) The* Titanic *graves at Fairview Cemetery as they look today.*

FLOATING RELICS

Not only bodies were recovered from the area of the disaster. Some wreckage was also found, including a delicately carved piece of oak paneling from above the forward entrance in the first-class lounge (below). A very similar motif of antique instruments can be seen in the photographs of the lounge on the Olympic (bottom left) and the lounge paneling today (bottom right).

(Above) Another fascinating find was an intact deck chair, now preserved along with the woodwork at the Maritime Museum of the Atlantic in Halifax. It is one of hundreds that were thrown or floated off the deck of the Titanic (top) as she sank.

(Far right) The Minia also recovered an oak newel post facing from one of the first-class staircases. The arrow on the photograph (right) shows a possible location.

179

London, May 3, 1912

BECAUSE OF SENATOR SMITH'S U.S. Senate inquiry, a number of crucial questions had been raised in the public's mind about the events of April 14 and 15, 1912. Chief among these was the matter of navigational negligence. Had Captain Smith — and by extension his most important passenger, Bruce Ismay — allowed the *Titanic* to sail too fast into ice-infested waters? There were other worrisome points as well. Was the "unsinkable" *Titanic* a safe ship, given how easily she sank and given the fact that she did not carry enough lifeboats to hold even a third of her full complement of passengers? Many wondered if certain passengers and crew had behaved in a proper manner. Should Ismay have left the ship? How did Sir Cosmo Duff Gordon, his wife, and her secretary end up in a lifeboat with only two other passengers? Were third-class passengers prevented from reaching the lifeboats? Perhaps most contentious of all was whether the *Californian* had seen but ignored the *Titanic's* distress signals.

Those who expected the British inquiry to resolve such issues would be disappointed. This investigation was not an attempt to get to the bottom of the story, but to sanitize it and remove its sting. The inquiry was a creature of the vested interests who had most to lose from a full investigation. It was conducted by the British Board of Trade (BOT) — the very government ministry responsible for Britain's outdated maritime safety laws, including the one that had rated the *Titanic* as having more lifeboats than required. Apart from protecting itself, the BOT had no interest in seeing the White Star Line found negligent. Any damage to White Star's reputation or balance sheet would be bad for British shipping — and there was considerable potential for both. Negligence on the part of the shipping company might pave the way for millions of dollars in damage claims and lawsuits that would tie up the courts for years, possibly break the White Star Line, and result in the loss of much of Britain's lucrative shipping traffic to the Germans and the French.

The commissioner presiding over the hearings was Lord Mersey, the seventy-two-year-old former president of the Admiralty, Probate, and Divorce Division of the High Court — an establishment man to the core. Sir Rufus Isaacs, a celebrated barrister, acted as chief counsel for the Board of Trade.

Even the choice of a site for the hearings seemed designed to dampen press and public interest. The London Scottish Drill Hall was a cavernous, drafty space with terrible acoustics — so bad that a large sounding board was placed in front of the dais reserved for the commissioner and his assessors. A huge model of the *Titanic* and a chart of the Atlantic dominated one side of the room, with spectators surrounding the tables placed in the center of the room for counsel and press.

On May 3, with the American inquiry still in progress and the principal witnesses not yet

The British inquiry was also known as the Mersey Commission after its presiding judge, Sir John Charles Bigham, Lord Mersey (inset).
The first witnesses called were surviving crew members. (Below) Crew survivors arrive home in Southampton before the inquiry.

London's Scottish Drill Hall has been replaced by a new building, but Caxton Hall (right), where the inquiry moved for its final session, still stands. Inside the new drill hall, the distinctive balconies from the old structure (far right), shown in the illustration of Bruce Ismay testifying (previous page), have been incorporated.

returned from the United States, proceedings began quietly. Fashionable London could not identify with the seamen and stokers who paraded to the witness stand in the early days. The interrogatory technique was, at best, rudimentary. In most instances a survivor's experiences were recited to him based on early depositions and then the witness simply agreed with the statement. There were exceptions, however. When one of the important players testified, many spectators were on hand and every person in the drill hall strained to follow the cut and thrust as the various lawyers asked their questions.

Sir Cosmo and Lady Duff Gordon had played no role in the *Titanic*'s fate, but their social standing combined with the controversy surrounding their conduct ensured that they would attract a large audience. Indeed, Friday, May 17, proved to be the most crowded day of the entire inquiry. Society turned out in force. The spectators included Margot Asquith, wife of the Prime Minister, Count Benckendorf, the Russian ambassador, several members of Parliament, and various aristocrats. In stark contrast to the fashionable apparel worn by the rich and titled was a group of *Titanic* stewardesses dressed in black.

Testifying on their own behalf gave the Duff Gordons the opportunity to turn the tide of public opinion in their favor. As Sir Cosmo took the stand, this was decidedly negative. The press had already made much of the fact that Sir Cosmo had offered each of the seven crewmen in lifeboat No. 1 five pounds to replace his kit, a promise he kept once on board the *Carpathia*. The money, coupled with the nearly empty lifeboat, made it tempting to infer that Sir Cosmo had purchased an almost private means of escape.

Sir Cosmo began calmly, describing how he and his wife came to be in the boat. "I then spoke to him [First Officer Murdoch] and I said, 'May we get into the boat?' and he said, 'Yes, I wish you would' or 'Very glad if you would' or some expression like that. There were no passengers at all near us then. He put the ladies in and helped me in."

When questioned about the suggestion that the lifeboat should return for swimmers, he denied ever hearing such a thing.

"Did it occur to you that with the room in your boat, if you could get to these people you could save some?" Sir Rufus Isaacs wanted to know.

"It is difficult to say what occurred to me," Sir Cosmo replied, seeming almost blasé. "Again, I was minding my wife, and we were rather in an abnormal condition, you know. There were many things to think about, but of course it quite well occurred to one that people in the water could be saved by a boat, yes."

Sir Cosmo then briefly described promising the men five pounds each to start a new kit, after which the session was adjourned for the weekend.

Monday, May 20, drew a London society crowd once again as Sir Cosmo was questioned by the other examiners. He stuck by his testimony of the previous Friday as the representatives of the various maritime unions took their turns.

The harshest interrogation came from W. D. Harbinson, counsel for the steerage passengers.

Almost immediately Lord Mersey had to caution him "Not to try to make out a case for this class or that class or another class, but to assist me in arriving at the truth." Harbinson was not so easily deterred. Within moments he was asking Sir Cosmo, "Was not this rather an exceptional time, twenty minutes after the *Titanic* sank, to make suggestions in the boat about giving away five pound notes?"

"No, I think not. I think it was a most natural time," Duff Gordon replied, again with almost appalling casualness. "Everything was quiet; the men had stopped rowing. The men were quite quiet lying on their oars doing nothing for some time, and then the ship having gone I think it was a natural enough remark for a man to make to me, 'I suppose you have lost everything?'"

"Would it not have been more in harmony with the traditions of seamanship that that should have been the time that you should have sug-

Sir Cosmo Duff Gordon is questioned about the events in lifeboat No. 1. The fact that his lifeboat was designed for forty people but held only twelve made the Duff Gordons the subject of criticism in the press. One verse reprinted in several papers included the lines, "Did you, / Sir Cosmo Duff Gordon, / On that night of tragedy / Behave as a gentleman or a coward?"

After Sir Cosmo (top) gave his testimony, it was Lady Duff Gordon's turn (inset and above) to take the stand. For "Lucile's" day in court the gallery was packed with society women in their finest spring outfits. To the New York Times *correspondent, it resembled "...a fashionable matinee in aid of a popular charity."*

gested to the sailors to have gone and tried if they could rescue any one?" Harbinson's question conveniently ignored the fact that the "traditions of seamanship" should have already been more apparent to the crew than to Sir Cosmo.

"I have said that I did not consider the possibility — or rather I should put it the possibility of being able to help anybody never occurred to me at all," Sir Cosmo rather weakly replied.

Now Harbinson moved in for the kill. "That is to say would I accurately state your position if I summed it up in this way, that you considered when you were safe yourselves that all the others might perish?"

"No, that is not quite the way to put it," Sir Cosmo responded.

Again Lord Mersey had to interject, pointing out to Harbinson that "The witness's position is bad enough." The applause that followed Mersey's remark served to emphasize his reprimand.

By the time the questioning finally ended, Sir Cosmo's jaunty self-confidence had crumbled, as had his reputation. It was now up to his wife, Lucile, to salvage the family honor.

Lady Duff Gordon made the most of her arrival on the stand. As a successful dress designer with "Lucile" stores in London and New York, she knew the right image to project. She wore black, including a huge hat and dark veil that made her seem tiny and frail. Her garb and demeanor clearly suggested that this was no cold, unfeeling aristocrat but a human being in mourning for the tragic victims of the *Titanic's* sinking.

Although the questioners treated Lady Duff

Gordon far more gingerly than her husband because she was a woman, she was not nearly so unwavering in her testimony. She denied hearing anything being said in the boat immediately after it had left the *Titanic*, until Sir Rufus Isaacs pointed out that she had told her solicitor she had heard someone suggest they pull away from the ship. She then allowed that, when speaking to her attorney, "I may have said so." She admitted to her mind being "hazy" about the sinking, and claimed that the cries and screams from the victims had occurred before the ship sank. In all, her testimony was brief, undoubtedly frustrating for the examiners, and dealt mostly with her denying an interview attributed to her by the Hearst newspapers.

By the end, she had not done her husband any harm, but neither had she done anything to help him.

The Duff Gordon sideshow mainly served to distract attention from the main issues. The testimony of the surviving officers and crew of the *Titanic* was expected to shed light on these, but overall these witnesses tended to help White Star's position. They were, after all, employees of the company and had to keep an eye to their future careers. The two key witnesses for the shipping line were Second Officer Charles Lightoller and White Star managing director Bruce Ismay. After the Duff Gordons' testimony concluded on May 20, several crewmen testified briefly. Then Lightoller took the stand. His testimony, detailed and exhaustive, lasted a day and a half.

As the only senior surviving officer of the *Titanic*, it fell to Lightoller to explain the navigational decisions taken by the captain and the

*On his way to give testimony,
Bruce Ismay (above, at right)
is accompanied by his wife,
Florence, and White Star director
Harold Sanderson.
Preceding Ismay on the stand was
Second Officer Charles Lightoller
(left, with pipe), who responded to
more than sixteen hundred
questions. Third Officer Herbert
Pitman, shown at left in
conversation with Lightoller just
after their return to England on the
Adriatic, also testified at the
investigation.*

officers above him. True to character, Lightoller now proved steadfast in defending his commander, by extension exonerating White Star of any negligence and the Board of Trade of any laxness in its regulations. He picked his way through a veritable minefield with all the skill and caution of a seasoned mariner.

Lightoller's interrogators had carefully reviewed his testimony at the U.S. inquiry, and many questions dealt with what he had said under oath to Senator Smith. Cleverly he repeatedly claimed he could not remember what he had said in New York, forcing his questioner to quote the record back to him. With his previous words fresh in his mind, Lightoller could be sure not to contradict himself and get the company into trouble.

The *Titanic*'s second officer also proved adept at avoiding a direct answer when it suited him. His fiercest adversary, Thomas Scanlan, who represented the National Sailors' and Firemen's Union, was determined to get him to admit that the *Titanic*'s officers were negligent in the hours leading up to the collision. First Scanlan questioned Lightoller about the unusual weather conditions. "This night you have described as being a particularly bad night for seeing icebergs. Is not that so?" This was indeed Lightoller's position, but he also maintained that the uniqueness of the weather conditions hadn't become apparent until after the collision. He simply replied, "I do not think I mentioned that word 'bad,' did I?"

Lightoller's canniness became apparent when Scanlan remarked, "Although there were abnormal difficulties you took no extra precautions whatever."

"Have I said so?" he replied.

Scanlan again attempted to pin Lightoller down: "In view of the abnormal conditions and of the fact that you were nearing ice at ten o'clock, was there not a very obvious reason for going slower?"

It was a yes or no question, but Lightoller managed to respond without using either. "Well, I can only quote you my experience throughout the last twenty-four years, that I have been crossing the Atlantic most of the time, that I have never seen the speed reduced."

"Is it not quite clear that the most obvious way to avoid it is by slackening speed?"

"Not necessarily the most obvious."

"Well, is it one way?" Scanlan was clearly frustrated.

"It is one way," Lightoller had to allow, adding, "Naturally, if you stop the ship you will not collide with anything."

Scanlan would not give up, nor would Lightoller back down. "What I want to suggest to you is that it was recklessness, utter recklessness, in view of the conditions which you have described as abnormal, and in view of the knowledge you had from various sources that ice was in your immediate vicinity, to proceed at 21 1/2 knots?"

"Then all I can say is that recklessness applies to practically every commander and every ship crossing the Atlantic Ocean," Lightoller replied.

"I am not disputing that with you, but can you describe it yourself as other than recklessness?"

"Yes," Lightoller replied. He would not, in any way, give Scanlan the satisfaction of making his point.

"Is it careful navigation in your view?"

Again Lightoller would not be cornered. "It is ordinary navigation, which embodies careful navigation."

None of the other examiners matched Scanlan's determination. Most merely corroborated Lightoller's previous testimony and questioned him regarding such details as the working of the boats, the Board of Trade inspection, the watertight doors, and other safety aspects of the ship. In the end his testimony served its purpose.

The public took Lightoller, the heroic second officer, at his word and concluded that the disaster was the result of abnormal weather conditions never before encountered by the officers on watch. Neither the White Star Line nor the Board of Trade could be held accountable.

Bruce Ismay was not called to testify until June 4. He wore a black suit with a white shirt. Still suffering under the strain he had experienced since the sinking, he now stood before a hall filled with people — something he had never found comfortable. In an attempt to cover his nervousness and keep from breaking down, he forced a weak smile to his face, which only made him appear indifferent to the seriousness of the occasion.

Like Lightoller, Ismay stuck by his American testimony. He was only a passenger; when Smith had handed him the *Baltic*'s message it was done without uttering a word. He stood by his story that he had met with Chief Engineer Joseph Bell on Thursday, April 11, and that he had wanted the ship's speed to be opened up on Monday or Tuesday, weather permitting. No one asked him why he wanted to wait, when the weather on Saturday and Sunday was perfect. By Monday the weather might well have changed and the opportunity to open her up on the maiden voyage lost. Elsewhere in his testimony, however, Ismay inadvertently implied that the ship's speed had been increased prior to the collision, testifying, "If a man can see far enough to clear ice, he is perfectly justified in going full speed." Despite this remark, he denied the newspaper accounts that had him telling Emily Ryerson on the Sunday that the ship was going to speed up to get out of the ice.

In all, Ismay categorically denied any knowledge of a plan for the *Titanic* to have been equipped with more lifeboats, but he could claim no knowledge regarding the actual navigation of the ship, despite the ice message that Captain Smith had handed him on Sunday afternoon. When it came to this subject, he had Lord Mersey on his side. At one point Sir Rufus Isaacs asked Ismay what right he had to order the chief engineer to open the ship up, without consulting the captain. Before Ismay could respond, Mersey cut in that Ismay had no right, but that the captain would know, hour by hour, what speed his ship was steaming. Mersey then insisted the matter be dropped. On another occasion, when W. D. Harbinson asked if the *Baltic* telegram was an invitation from Captain Smith for Ismay to express an opinion regarding the speed he felt the ship should take, Mersey cut him off, saying he must not ask such a question and that he should "ask questions about facts."

On only one point did Ismay disappoint Lord Mersey. Sir Rufus Isaacs was questioning the White Star managing director about the light toward which his lifeboat pulled, when Ismay responded, "If you will excuse my saying so, I do not think it was a steamer at all; I think it was a sailing ship we saw." Mersey quickly cut in, "Am I to understand that you do not think it was the *Californian?*"

"I am sure it was not," Ismay replied. The *Californian* was owned by the Leyland Line, one of International Mercantile Marine's companies.

"I am rather sorry to hear that," Mersey responded.

As the inquiry drew to a close, one man's testimony stood out as having captivated the public — that of Captain Lord of the *Californian*. The American inquiry had already pointed a finger at Captain Lord, so it wasn't surprising that Lord Mersey should have found in him the perfect scapegoat to draw attention away from the Board of Trade and the questions regarding the safety of England's large fleet of passenger ships. From the outset the commissioner showed hostility toward Lord, and very early in his testimony announced, "What is in my brain at the present

Sir Rufus Isaacs (center), chief counsel for the Board of Trade, and Solicitor-General Sir John Simon (right) leave the Scottish Drill Hall at the end of a day's proceedings. The British inquiry's public hearings ran for thirty-six days.

(Below) Alexander Carlisle, the former chairman of Harland and Wolff, testified that the number of lifeboats on board the Titanic had been far fewer than he, as one of the ship's designers, had originally proposed.

time is this, that what they saw [from on board the *Californian*] was the *Titanic*."

Captain Lord's testimony was not as extensive as Lightoller's or Ismay's would be, but it became apparent that this hardly mattered. Mersey had made his position apparent, and nothing Lord could say would change that. At one point Lord stated that he never heard either of the two officers on watch that night say that the light they could see from the *Californian* was a passenger ship. Mersey simply responded, "You do not give answers that please me."

Although Lord should have expected fierce questioning, given the reaction to his testimony at the American inquiry, he seems to have arrived on the witness stand remarkably ill-prepared to defend himself. He claimed to be certain that the ship seen from the *Californian* was not the White Star liner. He had seen it approach, and it was clearly not a large passenger steamer. Yet when Sir Rufus questioned Lord about the rockets apparently sent up from this ship, his answers were weak. At first he attempted to take the position that the rockets were an acknowledgment to his morse lamp. Isaacs wasn't about to accept this response.

"So far as you were concerned, you did not know at all what the rocket was for?" Isaacs asked.

"No," was Lord's simple reply, allowing himself to waver from his original position.

"And you remained in the chartroom."

"Yes, I remained in the chartroom."

"And you did nothing further."

"I did nothing further myself." Lord was easily falling into Isaacs' trap.

"If it was not a company's signal, must it not have been a distress signal?"

"If it had been a distress signal the officer on watch would have told me."

"I say," Isaacs repeated, leading Lord back toward the point he was trying to make, "if it

was not a company's signal, must it not have been a distress signal?"

"Well, I do not know of any other signals but distress signals that are used at sea."

In spite of his lapses, Lord continued to hold to his belief that the ship he saw was a small one like his own. He had made no attempt to wireless the vessel because his operator earlier had said that the only ship he had in the area was the *Titanic*, and this little steamer was clearly not the famous leviathan.

As could be expected, Lord Mersey's final report allowed the White Star Line and the British Board of Trade to escape virtually unscathed. Although he faulted Captain Smith for not altering course or slowing down, he exonerated him of any blame. He accepted Lightoller's argument that maintaining course and speed in good weather — simply trusting to lookouts to sight ice in time to avoid it — was common practice of long standing. Captain Smith had done "only that which other skilled men would have done in the same position." He did add, however, that "it is to be hoped that the last has been heard of this practice. What was a mistake in the case of the *Titanic* would without doubt be negligence in any similar case in the future."

Not surprisingly, Mersey recommended that lifeboat capacity be based on the maximum number of people a ship could carry rather than its tonnage. However, he sought to distract criticism of the Board of Trade's outdated regulations by making the extraordinary argument that since the *Titanic*'s lifeboats had been less than full, having more boats would *not* have saved more lives.

Not unexpectedly, Mersey found no fault in the treatment of third-class passengers. He held that Sir Cosmo Duff Gordon had not prevented lifeboat No. 1 from returning for swimmers. Nor did he censure Bruce Ismay. The White Star managing director had done all a man in his

THE MYSTERY OF THE THIRD SHIP

The controversy surrounding the Californian (top) and its captain, Stanley Lord (above), has been discussed and hotly debated for eighty years.

Although the American and British inquiries both condemned Captain Stanley Lord of the Leyland liner *Californian* for his failure to come to the *Titanic*'s rescue, his case continues to provoke controversy. Was the ship he and his officers saw that night actually the *Titanic*? If not, could there have been a third ship in the area, one seen both from the *Titanic* and from the *Californian*, which never identified itself and steamed off into the night while the *Titanic* sank? Whatever the answers to these questions, a careful sifting of the evidence shows serious holes in the case against Captain Lord.

On the evening of April 14, 1912, the *Californian* first saw a steamer's lights approaching shortly before 11:00 P.M. No one on the *Titanic* saw another steamer's lights until over an hour later, long after the liner had stopped. The *Californian* lay motionless in the water for the entire night, but many witnesses on the *Titanic* said the vessel they saw seemed to be approaching. This is supported by common sense: if the steamer appeared some time after the *Titanic* stopped, it must have been moving, however slow its speed. In a nutshell, although both the *Titanic* and the *Californian* were stopped dead in the water, the ship seen by each of them was in motion.

Other major discrepancies are equally difficult

(Left) Crew members of the Californian *who appeared at the British inquiry included Second Officer Stone and Apprentice Gibson (fourth and fifth from right), who were on watch when rockets were sighted. Their captain, Stanley Lord, also gave testimony at the inquiry and was photographed (right) leaving the Scottish Drill Hall.*

to explain away. Only one officer on the *Californian* thought the ship he saw was a passenger steamer, yet the *Titanic*, fifty percent larger than any other passenger ship afloat, should have been unmistakable at such close range. Captain Lord made no effort to radio the nearby ship because his wireless operator had told him the only vessel in the area in radio contact was the *Titanic*, and this ship was clearly not the huge liner. Captain Smith, believing his ship had less than an hour to survive, felt the steamer he saw was so close that he ordered his first few lifeboats to row over, drop off their passengers, and return.

The *Titanic*'s distress rockets rose high above the masts and rigging, bursting in a shower of colored balls, while the rockets seen from the *Californian* were all white, and rose no higher than halfway to the masthead light of the vessel in sight. On such a calm night, the sound of the *Titanic*'s

rockets should have been easily audible to any vessel in sight, yet those aboard the *Californian* heard nothing. Later, the survivors in the *Titanic*'s lifeboats heard the *Carpathia*'s rockets before that ship even came into view.

All this suggests that at least one other ship was in the vicinity of the *Titanic* that night, probably somewhere between her and the *Californian*. Certainly the sea was full of vessels. The next morning, several were visible while the *Carpathia* picked up survivors.

Over the years, various people have come forward to claim that the ship they were on that night was the mystery ship, naming the *Mount Temple*, the *Virginian*, the *Thistledhu*, and the most likely candidate, a Norwegian sailing ship, the *Samson*, which was sealing illegally in the area. Although more evidence may come to light, the mystery will likely never be solved.

However, defenders of Captain Lord, often known as "Lordites," now have significant new support for their position. A recently published report from England's Department of Transport partially exonerates the *Californian*'s captain. While it chastises Lord for not answering the distress flares he saw, it concludes, from the position of the *Titanic* wreck, that his ship was between seventeen and twenty miles away, out of sight of the sinking liner. Not only does this add weight to the case for the mystery ship, it confirms that even had Captain Lord acted at once, he could not have reached the *Titanic* in time. In broad daylight, able to see her way through the ice, it took the *Californian* two hours to reach the *Carpathia*. The first rocket was sighted at 12:40 A.M. by the *Californian*'s clocks. Two hours later, almost all those still struggling in the icy water would already have perished.

position could possibly do, and his presence in collapsible boat C did not prevent anyone else from being saved.

In his report, Lord Mersey directed the only real blame toward Captain Stanley Lord and the officers of the *Californian*. He concluded that the distance separating Lord's ship from the *Titanic* was between five and ten miles, and that it was indeed the *Titanic* the officers on the *Californian* had seen sending up rockets. "When she first saw the rockets the *Californian* could have pushed through the ice to the open water without any serious risk and so have come to the assistance of the *Titanic*. Had she done so she might have saved many if not all of the lives that were lost."

IN THE WAKE OF THE BRITISH INQUIRY, THE LIVES of the most prominent witnesses could never be quite the same. As a result of the unfavorable publicity, Captain Lord was forced to resign from the Leyland Line in August 1912. However, in January 1913 he was hired by the Nitrate Producers Steam Ship Company to command one of their vessels, and enjoyed a long and successful career. Sir Cosmo Duff Gordon's reputation never fully recovered from the stigma of his behavior, but if anything his wife thrived on the publicity. Later in 1912 she opened a Paris branch of "Lucile," and her business in that city soon flourished.

Charles Lightoller returned to the *Oceanic*, the ship on which he had served prior to the *Titanic*. He remained on board that vessel until early in World War I, when she struck a reef off the island of Foula and subsequently broke up. At the end of 1915 he finally received his own command, a torpedo boat, but this was during his wartime naval career. At war's end he realized that the White Star Line had no intention of giving a former officer of the *Titanic* his own ship, so he retired from the sea. For a number of years he ran a guest house in London, and later raised chickens. In World War II he used his own pleasure boat, the *Sundowner*, to assist in the evacuation of Dunkirk.

Of all those who survived the *Titanic* tragedy, Bruce Ismay may have suffered the most. Once safely in collapsible C, Ismay deliberately faced the other way as the *Titanic* sank, a gesture that could stand as a metaphor for the rest of his troubled life. Numerous editorials and cartoons lampooned the managing director of the White Star Line for having saved himself while the captain and most of the other men in first class went down with the ship. More than once in the years that followed, he must have regretted his own survival. He retired as planned from International Mercantile Marine in 1913, but the directorship of the White Star Line which he had hoped to retain, was denied him, and he was left with no active role in the company his father had built. He divided his time between homes in London and Ireland, and although he liked to be kept informed of shipping news, it was forbidden to mention the *Titanic* in his presence. His wife, Florence, would one day reflect that the disaster had ruined their lives.

In all, the American and British inquiries raised as many questions as they answered. With the recent revival of interest in the *Titanic*, which began with the publication of Walter Lord's *A Night to Remember* in 1955 and reached a peak with Dr. Robert Ballard's discovery of the wreck in 1985, many of these questions have been debated anew. The *Californian* controversy continues to rage (see page 190), with those defending Captain Lord calling themselves "Lordites."

Easier to dispel is the persistent argument that Captain Smith was negligent. The argument centers on the fact that the captain was speeding toward New York despite repeated warnings of dangerous ice ahead. However, as Lightoller and Lord Mersey pointed out, such behavior was com-

A 1912 newspaper cartoon (above) shows Bruce Ismay as the subject of the whispering and speculation that was to follow him for the rest of his life. A period book illustration (top) makes a similar point.

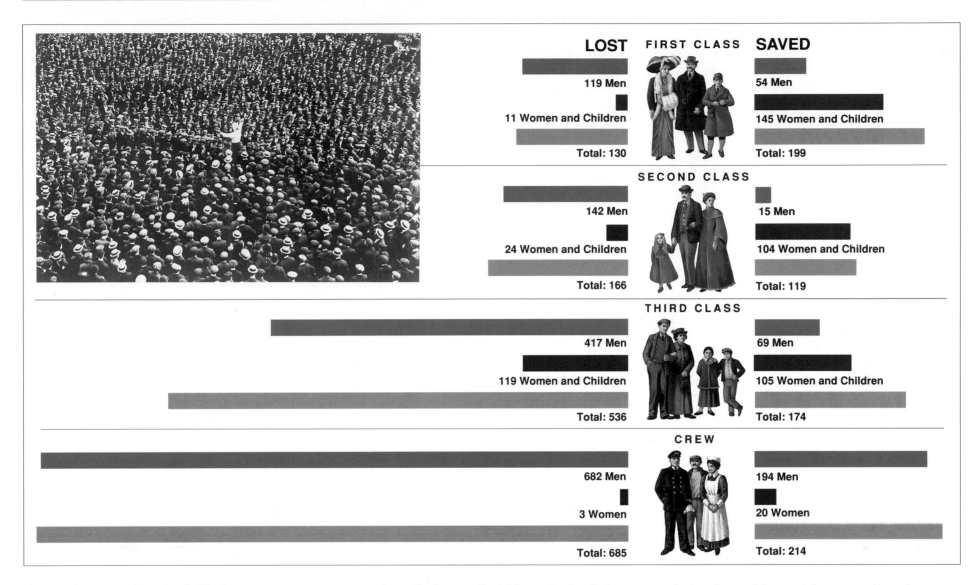

LOST   FIRST CLASS   **SAVED**

119 Men   54 Men

11 Women and Children   145 Women and Children

Total: 130   Total: 199

SECOND CLASS

142 Men   15 Men

24 Women and Children   104 Women and Children

Total: 166   Total: 119

THIRD CLASS

417 Men   69 Men

119 Women and Children   105 Women and Children

Total: 536   Total: 174

CREW

682 Men   194 Men

3 Women   20 Women

Total: 685   Total: 214

A crowd scene at London's Hyde Park (top) was used by the Illustrated London News *to demonstrate the sheer number of lives lost on the* Titanic. *The diagram (above) shows how the numbers of those lost and saved varied among the three classes and the crew. The figures used above are drawn from the report of the U.S. Senate investigation.*

monplace. In fact, to Smith's credit, he did turn the corner later than usual, putting him ten miles south of the normal April route. If Smith showed any negligence that night it was in being absent from the bridge at the most crucial time, when he knew his ship was about to enter the area of ice. From 9:00 P.M. until the collision, he made only one very brief appearance.

Some argue that Captain Smith could have done more after the ship began to sink, that he should have taken the mortally wounded *Titanic* and steamed toward the light in the distance. But Thomas Andrews had given the ship barely an hour to live, and much of this time was already lost by the time the light was sighted. Smith

obviously could not risk suspending the evacuation to steam toward a ship that was probably ten miles away. The *Titanic* was likely to sink before he got there.

Others maintain that Smith was right to remain stationary, but that all of the watertight doors should have been opened, causing the ship to flood more evenly and so remain more on an even keel. The bow would not have been pulled under so soon, they say, and the ship might even have remained afloat indefinitely. Perhaps, but Smith needed to keep the boiler and engine rooms dry as long as possible in order to keep power up so that the wireless and the pumps would continue to operate. Furthermore, flooding even a few boiler rooms goes against everything a ship's master is taught; namely to prevent flooding at all costs. No one knew the ship better than Thomas Andrews, its builder. Yet there is no evidence Andrews suggested any other course of action than the one Smith followed.

In short, Captain Smith's behavior that night was correct, if unimaginative and uninspiring. His reputation as a popular commander who went down with his ship has survived largely intact. In Smith's honor a statue was erected in the city of Lichfield, England, the seat of the diocese where Smith was born, sculpted by Lady Kathleen Scott and unveiled by his daughter in 1914. However, even at the time, one place did not share this reverence. This was Southampton, home to more victims than any other city in the world. In a port with numerous memorials to victims of the sinking, none commemorates Captain Smith, and the man with ultimate responsibility for the *Titanic*'s safety is not remembered kindly. A myth persists, due to Smith's presence at the Wideners' dinner party while the ship was approaching its fate, that the captain was drunk at the time of the collision. There is no evidence to support such a claim, but finding an aging sailor in Southampton who still believes it is not difficult.

If Captain Smith was not to blame, can some responsibility be assigned to the *Titanic*'s builders? Was she a safe ship in the first place? She had been designed with the latest in safety features: the best fire-detection apparatus, watertight doors, and bulkhead division. Had she been struck at the juncture of any two compartments, or hit head-on, she would have continued to float. The collision that occurred that night was an extraordinary one, with damage extending two hundred feet along the ship's hull. We will never know for sure, but we can surmise that the ship might have lasted longer, or not sunk at all, had her bulkheads extended up higher, had all her

watertight doors been closed automatically rather than just those below the passenger areas, and had she been built with a double hull. However, all of these advantages were later built into the *Titanic*'s sister ship, the *Britannic*, and yet when she struck a mine in the Aegean Sea in 1916, sustaining damage to a more compact area of the bow, she was lost in under an hour.

No shipwreck is complete without a treasure, and there is no shortage of speculation about the valuables the *Titanic* took to the bottom. Although Steward F. Dent Ray saw the pursers loading the contents of the first-class safes into canvas bags, these did not make it into any lifeboat. More likely the bags were placed back in the safes so that they could be removed quickly should the ship survive long enough. One has to question just how much valuable jewelry the average traveler carried in 1912. A woman's finest pieces were probably left at home, and there is no guarantee that what she brought on board was in the purser's safe at the time of the sinking. Sunday dinner had proved to be the most elegant of the voyage, and most of the jewelry worn that evening is now probably scattered throughout the remaining cabins or on the ocean floor.

More speculative still are the stories of a large gold shipment on board. One perpetuator of this legend was Storekeeper Frank Prentice, who years later would recall helping to bring gold and silver bars aboard. Researchers point out that the cargo manifest does not show such a shipment, though this fact does not necessarily eliminate the possibility that gold was carried. Gold shipments made as part of the balance of trade between England and the United States were regularly sent on Royal Mail Steamers as part of the mail, and so not charged as cargo. Unfortunately, the Bank of England seals its records for one hundred years. If indeed such a shipment existed, it was a secret kept from the news-hungry journalists of 1912.

Captain Edward J. Smith stands immortalized in bronze in his hometown of Lichfield, England. The plaque beneath him reads that he bequeathed to his countrymen "the memory and example of a great heart, a brave life and a heroic death."

The sinking of the Titanic *was described by seventeen-year-old survivor Jack Thayer (bottom) to* Carpathia *passenger L.D. Skidmore, who sketched these rough drawings. Of interest is the fact that they show the* Titanic *breaking in two before sinking rather than going down intact.*

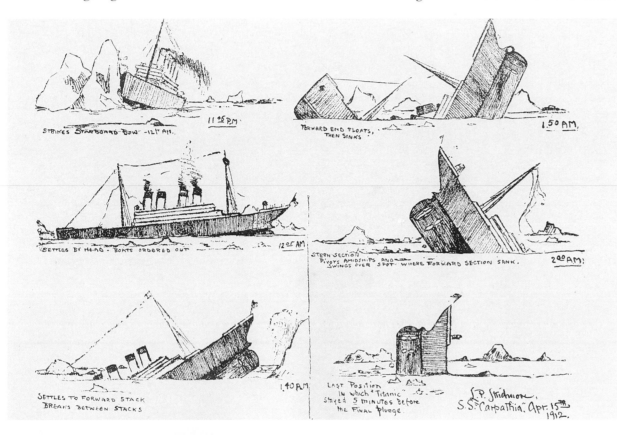

At least one *Titanic* question was answered with the discovery of the wreck in 1985. Did the ship sink in one piece? The two passengers who wrote books about the sinking immediately afterward, Colonel Archibald Gracie and Lawrence Beesley, both said so. Beesley claimed he saw the ship sink intact, while Gracie, who was underwater at the time, felt that the forward funnel breaking off must have created the illusion of the ship's hull separating. Many newspaper accounts of the day carried interviews with survivors who described the ship breaking in two, a story corroborated by many of the crewmen who testified at the British inquiry. Nonetheless, historians chose to believe Beesley and Gracie. Only the discovery of the bow, lying 1,970 feet from the stern on the ocean bottom, buried this controversy for good.

Of all the *Titanic* issues that will never be resolved, the fate of First Officer Murdoch remains one of the most tantalizing. Various passengers and crew described seeing Murdoch shoot a man who was trying to get into the last boat. Some claimed he then shot himself. Others, such as Hugh Woolner, stated that the first officer had only fired into the air to warn off a crowd just before the boat was lowered. Nellie Becker, who spent each day on the *Carpathia* discussing the sinking with other survivors, met no one who had actually seen anyone shot. And Second Officer Lightoller testified that he saw the first officer still working at collapsible A just before the bow began to plunge.

Murdoch had been demoted from chief officer just before the *Titanic*'s maiden voyage, and it was he who stood on the bridge when the *Titanic* struck the iceberg, so it is tempting to imagine his anguished, suicidal state of mind as the ship sank. Certainly Lightoller's testimony can be discounted — he may well have been attempting to protect the reputation of a fellow White Star officer, as well as that of his employers. It seems clear that some shots were fired, probably by Murdoch. Whether any were aimed and hit their mark, we will never know. First Officer Murdoch's body was not among those recovered, nor was any corpse found to have been shot. The only recovered body found to yield any evidence of a firearm was that of Michel Navratil, a second-class passenger who had kidnapped his two sons from his estranged wife in Nice and was bringing them to America. In his pocket was a fully loaded revolver.

Part of the lure and mystery of the *Titanic* will always be its unanswered questions. Would a different captain have avoided the iceberg? Could the ship have been prevented from sinking? What kind of gash did the iceberg cause in the hull? Ironically, the discovery of the wreck in 1985 solved some of the mysteries, but it created others. More than anything, the discovery proved that the *Titanic* has become a permanent object of fascination for millions.

Chapter Ten

DISCOVERY

July 14, 1986

ON JULY 14, 1986, THERE appeared in the darkness at the bottom of the north Atlantic several bright lights, which cast their beams across the muddy ocean floor. The lights belonged to a small three-man submersible, *Alvin*. Suddenly the mud gave way to a dark mass rising abruptly from the bottom. It was the bow of the wreck of the *Titanic*.

The tiny sub paused briefly, moved to the port side, then rose up along the hull past intact portholes and huge fingers of rust, finally coming to rest on what was once a wooden deck just forward of the mast from which Lookout Frederick Fleet had spotted the iceberg. Nearly seventy-five years after the tragic events of April 1912, Martin Bowen, Ralph Hollis, and Dr. Robert Ballard of the Woods Hole Oceanographic Institution were, in effect, the first to board the *Titanic* since her maiden voyage.

Alvin then lifted off and drifted aft past the mast, now fallen backward and stretching above the well deck where crewmen and third-class passengers had once playfully kicked shards of iceberg. Then the submersible finally settled near the location of the ship's bridge. All that remained of it and the wheelhouse was the telemotor which had once held the ship's wheel that Robert Hichens had spun "hard a' starboard" in a desperate attempt to avoid the collision.

As the submersible moved aft, it passed the opening left by the forward funnel when it crashed into the water. Then *Alvin* hovered over the gaping hole where the dome over the first-class Grand Staircase had once been. Next it dropped down alongside the port A-deck promenade, where the cream of New York and Philadelphia

society had waited to enter lifeboat No. 4. As the *Alvin* continued aft, its lights reflecting in the still-intact glass of stateroom windows, it suddenly struck something, launching a cascade of rust and silt. The obstacle proved to be a davit once used to launch lifeboat No. 8 and now extending over the edge of the deck. Finally, due to worsening weather topside and a problem with its batteries, *Alvin* began the two-and-a-half-hour ascent to the research vessel *Atlantis II* waiting at the surface.

Alvin's dramatic encounter with the *Titanic* culminated many years of dreaming and planning and several unsuccessful attempts to locate the wreck. The idea of finding this famous sunken ship, of photographing or even salvaging her, could be traced back almost to the moment the *Titanic* first disappeared beneath the surface. That very year, the Astor, Guggenheim, and Widener families contacted the Merritt and Chapman Wrecking Company regarding the possibility of salvage. As early as 1914, in an article on underwater photography, the magazine *Popular Mechanics* predicted that one day the children of the victims might see photographs of the wreck.

But it was not until fifty years later that technological developments, combined with a renewed interest in the *Titanic*, made a search-and-salvage venture possible. Various schemes were proposed, some incredibly farfetched. One suggestion involved filling the ship with Ping-Pong balls to bring her bobbing to the surface — forgetting, of course, that even table tennis balls fall victim to underwater pressure. Other ideas included attaching to the hull bags filled with helium, or even gasoline.

Most of those who dreamed of finding and raising the *Titanic* seem to have had little idea

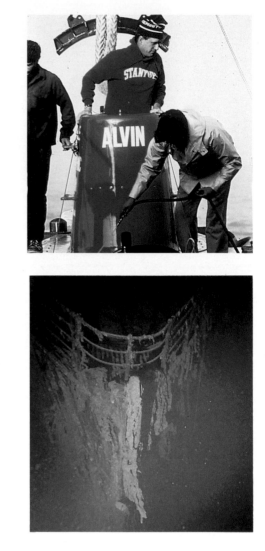

(Top) Robert Ballard emerges from the turret of the submersible Alvin *after his first descent to the* Titanic *on July 13, 1986. The next day he explored the bow section of the wreck and photographed the liner's rust-enshrouded prow (above).*

When Robert Ballard first glimpsed the Titanic *(above)*, it looked like a wall of steel rising from the ocean floor. *(Left)* During a descent to the wreck site, he communicates with the research ship Atlantis II, *while pilot Dudley Foster checks the submarine's depth. (Top right) Formations Ballard dubbed "rusticles" hang over the porthole to a first-class stateroom. (Bottom right) A davit that once lowered lifeboat No. 8 now lies flat on the deck, partly suspended over the port side.*

(Left) Rusticles hang from two large bitts on the forward deck.

For years prior to the discovery of the wreck, many had dreamed of finding the ship lying in one piece (top) on the ocean floor. This dream led Jack Grimm (above) to sponsor three expeditions in search of the Titanic. Here he holds a press conference following his 1981 expedition.

of what they would do with the ship once she was brought to the surface, beyond looting her of any valuable contents. Some envisioned the resurrected leviathan as a floating museum — an idea scoffed at by at least one self-appointed expert as requiring too much paint to be financially feasible.

All these schemes were based on the false assumption that the hull remained in one piece on the ocean floor and that it was in sufficiently good condition to be raised without disintegrating. For years Titanic aficionados dreamed of a wreck untouched by decay. Experts theorized that there would be no oxygen at the Titanic's depth and that the temperature would be cold enough to have prevented the decomposition of wood, fabric, and perhaps even human bodies. All would be as it had been on the night of April 14, 1912 — food still in the galleys, luggage still in the staterooms — a perfect time capsule of the Edwardian era.

Despite the speculation, no salvage operation left port until July 1980, when the 180-foot research vessel H.J.W. Fay sailed from Port Everglades, Florida, with a crew of thirty-eight, including twenty scientists and writer William Stephenson, best-selling author of A Man Called Intrepid. The expedition was the brainchild of film producer Mike Harris, but its chief backer and most colorful participant was Jack Grimm, a Texas oil millionaire with a penchant for tilting at windmills. He had already financed ambitious searches for the Loch Ness Monster, Big Foot, and Noah's Ark.

Since Grimm's target this time was something known definitely to exist, he was fiercely determined to succeed. He had hired top people, and his ship was equipped with a sophisticated side-scan sonar (able to pick out large objects on the ocean floor) as well as a magnetometer to determine whether any promising sonar targets were metal. When and if these two criteria were

met, underwater cameras would be lowered to make a definite identification.

Grimm and his colleagues had studied the historical record and were sure that the Titanic lay within an area bounded by 41° 55' north latitude, 41° 35' north latitude, 50° 20' west longitude, and 49° 55' west longitude. They based this area on the CQD position, allowing for variations in the dead-reckoning position due to the Titanic's speed, her drift after the collision, and additional drift on her way to the bottom. They also took into consideration the Californian's reported position, and her possible distance from the White Star liner.

Unfortunately, the expedition was plagued from the start by stormy weather. Fifty-mile-an-hour winds and twelve-foot swells almost immediately caused the loss of the magnetometer. After forty-five days of arduous searching, the expedition had identified fourteen possible targets, one of which was the length and width of the Titanic's hull, but this lay in a submarine canyon. Continued bad weather prevented the lowering of the camera equipment, and finally, with dwindling supplies of food and fuel, the team was forced to return to the United States.

Jack Grimm, however, did not give up easily. In July 1981, he and Harris returned on board the 174-foot Gyre, which was equipped with an improved side-scan sonar and a new magnetometer. Feeling certain that this time they would find the ship, the expedition included a film crew and actor James Drury to do on-board narration. First they would inspect the fourteen targets they had identified in 1980. If these proved to be geological features, they would continue the search. Now more than ever convinced that the Titanic had landed on the ocean floor intact, they began their search.

To Grimm's chagrin, the ship-sized object in "Titanic Canyon" was not made of metal, and the other thirteen targets likewise proved to be rocky outcrops rather than pieces of man-made wreckage. In all, a thirty-square-mile area was scanned using the magnetometer and sonar, though the expedition largely covered the same ground that had been searched in 1980. Finally, with time running out and nothing to show for the millions of dollars spent, the video cameras were lowered. Everyone on board knew this was a longshot, but they had nothing to lose. The camera did find something — the edge of a large object that was shaped roughly like a ship's propeller blade.

Without positive identification of the propeller, the second Grimm expedition could not be considered a success. Having run out of time, the *Gyre* was brought home. Two years later Grimm returned with the research vessel *Robert D. Conrad*. The area where the "propeller" had been sighted was searched with a side-scan sonar, but the *Titanic* was nowhere to be found. Fighting winds between thirty and forty knots, and swells as high as thirty feet, the expedition ended. Neither Grimm nor Harris would ever have the opportunity to mount another search.

It was not a treasure hunter who eventually found the *Titanic*. Dr. Robert Ballard, an underwater geologist from the Woods Hole Oceanographic Institution in Massachusetts, had dreamed of finding the ship as early as 1973, with the intent of using the wreck as a subject for testing undersea photography. For years Ballard had pursued the venture, but he was unable to find the support — both financial and scientific — that he needed. During that period, however, he worked at developing *Argo*, a deep-towed, remotely controlled camera sled, as well as *Jason*, a robot submarine that would also carry camera and lighting equipment. Ballard's sophisticated technology ultimately brought his plan to fruition. The United States Navy agreed to fund a three-week test of *Argo* as part of a search for the *Titanic*.

In the summer of 1985 all the pieces were in place. On July 5, a joint expedition by the Woods Hole Oceanographic Institution and the French oceanographic organization IFREMER arrived in the search area aboard the French vessel *Le Suroit*. Like Grimm they planned to search for the wreck using a side-scan sonar. To determine the search area they began with the spot where the *Carpathia* had recovered the lifeboats. These boats, based upon the *Californian*'s log of the currents that morning, had to have drifted south-southeast from where they had been when the ship foundered. Consequently, the expedition believed, the *Titanic* was somewhere to the north.

Added to this theory were a few assumptions. If the *Titanic* was not going quite as fast as its officers had thought, or if the current was stronger than its officers assumed in calculating the dead-reckoning position, the ship might be farther east than Grimm had believed. Ballard's initial search area was wholly contained within Grimm's 1980 quadrant, but it was much smaller and located entirely to the east of the *Titanic*'s distress position.

During a month on site the French ship covered three-fourths of the search area without turning up any object big enough to be the *Titanic*. Strong currents and bad weather made a systematic search difficult, and when *Le Suroit*'s time was up, the task was continued by the Woods Hole research vessel *Knorr*. Ballard, the American co-leader, opted at this point to abandon the sonar search strategy used by the French for a visual exploration using his underwater camera vehicle, *Argo*. This meant looking not for a large piece of wreckage but for a roughly one-mile-long debris trail that would have been deposited as the ship sank to the bottom.

With limited time and only one small section in the extreme eastern corner of the original search area yet to be investigated — a small swatch missed by the French because of bad weather — Ballard and his co-leader, Jean-Louis Michel, had

Six weeks of sonar tracking on the French ship Le Suroit *(top) in 1985 revealed no sign of the lost liner. Discouragement shows (above) on the faces of Ballard and the French team leader, Jean-Louis Michel.*

The discovery of one of the
Titanic's *giant boilers (above) led*
to jubilation (below) in the Knorr's
control room. In 1986 Ballard
returned to explore the wreck with
the submersible Alvin *(top right)*
and the underwater robot Jason
Junior *(bottom right).*

all but given up hope. They expanded their search area to the east of where the *Titanic's* lifeboats had been found and began laboriously "mowing the lawn" with their camera as time quickly ran out. Then, shortly after midnight on September 1, fragments of man-made wreckage appeared on the *Knorr's* video screens. At 1:05 A.M. a boiler that could only have belonged to the *Titanic* filled the screens. As it turned out, the wreck was in the tiny corner of the original search area missed by the French and just barely within the eastern boundary of Jack Grimm's 1980 search quadrant.

Armed with miles of videotape and thousands of still photographs, Ballard returned to Woods Hole to a tumultuous welcome and enormous international publicity. The *Titanic* had made him a superstar overnight, and as a result he was able to mount a second expedition with the sole

purpose of exploring the wreck and the surrounding debris field while testing the prototypes of his underwater video technology. Over a period of twelve days, ten dives were made to the ship in the submersible *Alvin*, with the remote camera *Jason Junior* taking video footage of the wreck. This undersea exploration yielded a much fuller picture of the wreck, and the story of what had become of the *Titanic* after she disappeared beneath the surface began to unfold.

After the stern rose out of the water the ship broke in two — at the surface, as many witnesses reported — separating between the third and fourth funnels. The section of the ship aft of this point contained the engine rooms and was simply too heavy to remain intact. The break occurred at a weak point in the structure caused by the large open spaces, including the aft Grand Staircase, in the areas above. As the ship plunged

The massive damage sustained by the Titanic's stern section is most evident in this view (above) looking aft on the starboard side. It appears as if the decks collapsed down on each other upon impact with the bottom, causing the hull to literally blow apart. On the right, the high-pressure cylinders from the reciprocating engines still stand upright. The Ballard team photographed hundreds of objects from the ship lying near the stern, including a bronze deck-bench frame (right) and a rust-draped bathtub (far right).

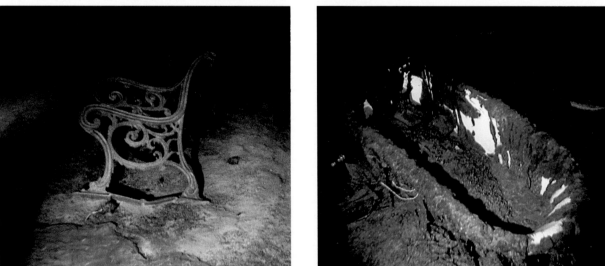

A battered soup tureen (above left), a copper saucepan (above right), the statuette (right) from the first-class lounge fireplace (see page 47), and a painted metal footboard from a first-class stateroom (below) were among the thousands of objects that spilled out of the ship when it sank.

The Titanic's *severed stern (at left) lies 1,970 feet away from the more intact bow section. The bow and stern rest on a gently sloping area of ocean floor, facing in opposite directions.*

to the bottom, the three remaining funnels were swept away, taking most of the rigging with them. As cables dragged along the boat deck, they knocked away most of the davits and a good deal of other equipment. The bow, still structurally intact, glided to the bottom at an angle, striking nose first and burying sixty feet into the silt. As this part of the ship settled on the bottom, plates buckled and ruptured along both sides. The aft part of the bow bent slightly, while the forepeak remained buried in the mud at a sharper angle.

Meanwhile, the stern section, which, unlike the bow, had not fully filled with water, plunged straight down. The incoming water forced out the remaining air, wreaking havoc and damage. The poop deck, which had formed the roof over the third-class lounge and smoking room, was torn open and folded back onto itself. The stern hit the bottom hull first, landing with such force that the decks accordioned down onto one another, the sides of the hull bulging outward.

Scattered all around the area was a huge debris field littered with objects that fell from the ship as she broke in two. Huge sections of hull plating and a main piece of decking (believed to be from the galleys which once extended the width of the ship) landed only a short distance away, together with cargo cranes, bedsprings, dishes, bottles, basins, window frames from public rooms, light fixtures, balustrades, and hundreds of other objects.

Contrary to many expectations, the deep ocean did not preserve the *Titanic* from decay. Softer materials such as cloth, paper, and most woods were eaten away by deep-sea organisms. The wood decking and furniture were nearly all gone, as were the human remains that were once scattered about the bottom. Only a few pairs of shoes, spared by the sea, indicated where bodies had once rested. Huge fingers of rust extended from exposed metal, almost covering the hull. Nonetheless, the wreck remained in a remarkable

(Above) Alvin *sits on the devastated bridge area while* Jason Junior *illuminates the crow's nest on the fallen foremast. With its wheelhouse washed away, the bridge today (left) is a changed scene from how it looked in 1912 (see page 81). The bronze telemotor (right) that once held the ship's wheel now stands alone near the crumbled wooden foundation for the forward wheelhouse wall.*

On Ballard's third dive he landed beside the collapsed roof that once held the glass dome over the first-class staircase. He then sent Jason Junior down the staircase shaft as far as B-deck. (Right) The underwater robot illuminates traces of former elegance — a light fixture still dangling from its cord and the carved oak bases of some of the pillars. A photograph of the light fixture (below) shows that it has sprouted a feathery sea pen.

207

state of preservation — a fascinating underwater museum.

Despite attempts by the United States Congress to prevent the wreck from being looted, a 1987 expedition involving American and European investors and the French co-discoverers IFREMER dove on the site in the submersible *Nautile*. Its mechanical arms plucked hundreds of objects from the debris field and the wreck itself. These included bottles, dishes, light fixtures, an empty safe, luggage, and a statue of a cherub from the aft Grand Staircase. Even the crow's-nest bell was retrieved. As it was pulled from

the mast, the crow's nest itself collapsed.

The expedition drew an outcry of protest from around the world. Of the few remaining survivors, Eva Hart, who had been seven years old in 1912 and was now a retired welfare officer and justice of the peace living near London, became the most outspoken. "To bring up those things from a mass sea grave just to make a few thousand pounds shows a dreadful insensitivity and greed," she explained to reporters. "The grave should be left alone. They're simply going to do it as fortune hunters, vultures, pirates!"

The United States Senate responded by passing a bill, sponsored by Lowell Weicker of Connecticut, which forbade the sale or display for profit of any *Titanic* salvage in the United States. However, this could not stop the broadcast from Paris in October 1987 of "Return to the *Titanic...Live!*" — a tasteless television production hosted by Telly Savalas. During the show a valise recovered from the debris field by *Nautile* was opened. Inside were coins, currency, and jewelry, some of it bearing the initials RLB and apparently belonging to Richard L. Beckwith of New York. One of the items, a pendant set with a small diamond, bore the ironic inscription, "This be your lucky star." Restoration of the artifacts by use of electrolysis was immediately begun. Those involved with the expedition indicated that the artifacts would be returned to the families of the original owners, but so far little, if any, effort has been made to do so. Neither did the 1987 expedition appear to treat the wreck as an archaeological site, carefully documenting the location of each artifact. No such documentation, should it exist, has ever been made available.

Stung by the criticism, and in an attempt to give their dive more scientific legitimacy, the leaders of the 1987 expedition unveiled a new theory about the sinking of the ship. The ruptures on each side of the bow were caused by an explosion, they hypothesized, not an iceberg. The coal-bunker fire that had burned early in the voyage had somehow caused a detonation which sank the ship. The theory ignored the numerous accounts by both the passengers and crew who had witnessed the iceberg. It also overlooked all testimony by the survivors, none of whom had heard or felt anything resembling an explosion until the ship broke in half and was already foundering. The holes now visible on the hull are located where the plates ruptured when the

Thousands of White Star artifacts similar to these (left) were raised from the Titanic *wreck in 1987. High-quality images were all that were taken from the site in 1992 by a Russian/Canadian/U.S. expedition (right). (Above) The Russian submersible* Mir 2 *is prepared for launching from RV* Akademik Keldysh *while the still camera on* Mir 1 *(far right) is tested.*

bow bent downward after striking the bottom. These are in the cargo areas and above the waterline. Not only was there no known cargo that could have caused an explosion, no water could have entered the ship this high up.

The backers of the fourth and most recent voyage to the wreck in June 1991 had clearly learned the lessons of adverse publicity. This primarily joint Soviet and Canadian expedition spent nearly three weeks on site and shot over 40,000 feet of 70-millimeter film for a giant-screen IMAX documentary. Two twin submersibles, the *Mir 1* and *Mir 2*, each capable of holding three people, made seventeen dives, spending a total of 140 hours on the sea bottom. The result is a remarkable film which, when seen on a huge IMAX screen, gives viewers the feeling they are actually at the bottom of the sea, exploring the most famous shipwreck on earth.

In addition to filming the *Titanic*, scientists on this latest expedition used the opportunity to study deep-sea life as well as the environmental processes active at that depth. Twenty-four animal species and four fish species were documented at the site, including crabs, starfish, sponges, anemones and large rat-tail fish. In addition, the Soviet submersibles used their articulated arms to push 30-centimeter-long tubes into the floor of the ocean to retrieve core samples. These will be used to study the capacity of sea-bottom sediments to absorb man-made wastes.

No doubt future expeditions will find their way to the *Titanic*. Now that the wreck has been found, the fascination of her story seems only to have grown. Robert Ballard himself hopes to return to the site to do live television broadcasts to schoolchildren. Other oceanographers will likely see the *Titanic* as a wonderful opportunity to give their scientific research public appeal. One hopes, however, that all future visits will respect the grave site and leave it untouched for future generations to rediscover and explore.

Chapter Eleven

THE TITANIC LEGACY

August, 1992

THERE HAVE BEEN WORSE MARITIME disasters since that early morning in 1912, but the story of the *Titanic* has outlasted them all and, with the recent discovery of the wreck, interest in the ship shows no sign of abating. There are many reasons why this ghost haunts us still. Above all, however, is the simple power of the story that was played out in the mid-Atlantic — a story as good as any fiction.

The largest and most luxurious ocean liner in the world sets out on her maiden voyage carrying the wealth and society of two continents. Among her passengers are the managing director of the company that owns the ship, and her builder. Everyone on board is awed by this wonderful new liner's size and seeming invincibility.

As the voyage unfolds, ominous warnings of dangerous ice ahead are all but ignored by the supremely confident captain and his crew. Then, just before midnight on the fifth night out, with most of the passengers already in bed and the ocean as smooth as glass, the ship hits an iceberg. For the next two and a half hours, as the great liner slowly sinks, an excruciating human drama unfolds. Ordinary people perform acts of bravery and self-sacrifice, and the full range of human strength and weakness is on display. It is a scenario in which we cannot resist imagining ourselves, as we try to decide what we would have done and how we would have reacted.

Few events have inspired as many words, both written and spoken, as the loss of the *Titanic*. In the immediate aftermath of the disaster, the press coverage was enormous. Then the American and British inquiries kept the story on the front page for months. Ministers rushed to their pulpits to affix moral and spiritual blame. Legislators and journalists called for reforms. Hastily written books such as *The Sinking of the Titanic and Great Sea Disasters* soon appeared to cash in on the public interest, although more serious works were eventually published: Filson Young's *Titanic*, Lawrence Beesley's *The Loss of the Titanic*, and Colonel Archibald Gracie's *The Truth About the Titanic*.

In those early days people seemed most captivated by stories that revealed either cowardice or heroism. Like Bruce Ismay and Sir Cosmo Duff Gordon, many of the men who were saved found their reputations irreparably damaged. Those who stoically went down with the ship were revered. Given that in those Edwardian days the wealthy and the titled were celebrities equivalent to our modern movie and rock stars, it is not surprising that many writers concentrated on the nobility and heroism of certain first-class passengers.

Author and publisher Elbert Hubbard was one such writer. He argued that despite their wealth, which had made them accustomed to privilege, the real heroes of the tragedy were the first-class passengers who willingly stepped aside to let others live. "The Strauses, Stead, Astor, Butt, Harris, Thayer, Widener, Guggenheim, Hays — I thought I knew you, just because I had seen you, realized somewhat of your able qualities, looked into your eyes and pressed your hands, but I did not guess your greatness. These dead have not lived and died in vain. They have brought us all a little nearer together — we think better of our kind."

Hubbard paid particular attention to Isidor and Ida Straus, the elderly couple who had gone down together. "Mr. and Mrs. Straus, I envy you that legacy of love and loyalty left to your children and grandchildren. The calm courage that was

The Olympic *and the* Titanic *were both featured in picture postcards, and the sinking spurred the creation of many commemorative cards. Today, these are valued by collectors as mementos of the disaster and evocations of an era.*

WHATEVER HAPPENED TO LORAINE ALLISON?

On January 21, 1909, several plate-layers working on the North London Railway made a grisly discovery — the tiny body of a baby boy, apparently thrown from a train the night before. Within weeks, Alice Mary Cleaver of Tottenham was arrested for the murder of her own child. Although she maintained that she had given the baby to a "Mrs. Gray" of an orphanage in Kilburn, no such woman or institution could be found. Alice was convicted of her crime but the jury recommended leniency and she eventually went free. By April 1912, she was on board the *Titanic* working as a nurse for the Hudson Allison family of Montreal. On the night of the disaster, Alice managed to save herself and the Allison's infant son, Trevor. But two-year-old Loraine Allison perished with her parents.

In the fall of 1940, a Mrs. Loraine Kramer appeared on the American radio program, "We the People," stating that she was Loraine Allison. She claimed that as the *Titanic* was sinking she had been handed to a man name Hyde who had taken her to safety and then raised her in the American Midwest. Mrs. Kramer was soon in touch with relatives on both sides of Loraine's family. Her claim was not welcomed by Mrs. Lillian Allison of Montreal, the widow of Hudson Allison's brother, George. As guardians of Trevor Allison, whom Alice Cleaver had rescued from the *Titanic,* George and Lillian had inherited the bulk of the Allison estate when Trevor had died of ptomaine poisoning in 1929. If Loraine Kramer was Loraine Allison, she

Loraine Allison with baby Trevor.

stood to benefit at Lillian's expense. Loraine Kramer insisted, however, that all she wanted was to have a family like everyone else. To support her claim she had some unusually clear memories from the age of two and a half, and several pieces of family jewelry. (These were sent to Bess Allison's sister who found them to be cheap imitations.) She also claimed possesion of a diary that her rescuer, Mr. Hyde,

had kept over the years.

Before long, Loraine Kramer was represented by a lawyer, Arthur Flynn of Morrisburg, Ontario, and with his "research" into the case, the story became even more farfetched. The Mr. Hyde who had saved Loraine was none other than Thomas Andrews, the ship's builder. He and the little girl had shared the doctor's cabin on the *Carpathia* with Bruce Ismay who had then paid Andrews to "disappear" so that he could not testify that the *Titanic* was traveling too fast. Over the years, as Loraine and Andrews had moved from town to town, they had been visited by Ismay, by George Allison (who was also paying Hyde/Andrews to keep Loraine away from the Allison money), and by Andrews' sister, a "Mrs. Gray." The revealing clue here is that "Mrs. Gray" is the same pseudonym that Alice Cleaver had invoked at her trial in 1909.

Lillian Allison claimed that she had been in touch with Alice Cleaver and that the former nurse had confirmed that Loraine was not rescued from the *Titanic,* but no letter or even a current address for Alice Cleaver was ever produced. It would seem more likely — from the "Mrs. Gray" connection — that it was Alice Cleaver who had supplied Loraine Kramer with Allison memories. Nevertheless, the would-be Loraine Allison persisted with her claim for ten years until the death of her lawyer, Arthur Flynn, in 1951. She then reported that all his files, including the "Andrews" diary, had been destroyed in a fire. Eventually she moved west and the Allison family never heard from her again.

(Above) This memorial to the Titanic's *stewards was unveiled in Southampton on July 27, 1915. (Above right) In April of the previous year, a ceremony in Southampton's East Park dedicated a monument to the ship's engineers (see pages 210 – 211). The death on the* Titanic *of Charles Hays (left), president of Canada's Grand Trunk Railway, caused the cancellation of celebrations for the opening of the railway's new Chateau Laurier Hotel in Ottawa.*

yours all your long and useful career was your possession in death. To pass out as did Mr. and Mrs. Isidor Straus is glorious. Few have such a privilege." Ironically, three years later Hubbard and his wife were passengers on another liner, the *Lusitania*, when it was torpedoed by a German submarine. Like the Strauses, they were lost at sea together.

In the immediate aftermath of the disaster, the entire world seemed caught up in the heroism of those who died on the *Titanic*. Countless plaques, statues, fountains, and buildings were erected in memory of the sinking. Among the many memorials in Southampton, England, there is a huge statue celebrating the engineering staff, all of whom were lost; a fountain dedicated to the victims among the crew; and a bronze plaque, cast from the *Titanic*'s spare propeller, honoring the ship's postal workers.

For over fifty years the Titanic Memorial Lighthouse sat atop New York's Seamen's Church Institute before being moved to the South Street

Seaport Museum. In Washington, D.C., Henry Bacon, the designer of the Lincoln Memorial, created an impressive monument to the men lost; it includes an eighteen-foot-high statue of a man with arms outstretched.

Of all the memorials throughout the world, the largest and most lavish is the Widener Memorial Library at Harvard University, erected by Mrs. George D. Widener in honor of her son, Harry. Many other individuals have been honored as well. The ship's builder is remembered in his hometown of Comber, Northern Ireland, by the Thomas Andrews, Jr. Memorial Hall. Both Molly Brown's home in Denver, Colorado, and her birthplace in Hannibal, Missouri, have been preserved for the public. Major Archibald Butt, President Taft's military aide, had a bridge named for him at his birthplace of Augusta, Georgia, and a fountain in Washington, D.C., dedicated to his memory and to the memory of artist Francis Millet, Butt's friend and a fellow passenger. Godalming, England, has a memorial garden in memory of Wireless Operator Jack Phillips, and schoolchildren in Dalbeattie, Scotland, still compete for a writing prize named after First Officer William Murdoch.

Of greater significance than buildings or monuments is the *Titanic*'s legacy of safer sea travel. Spurred by the revelations at the American and British inquiries, many commentators called for major changes in safety regulations. The novelist, Joseph Conrad, who had spent much of his life at sea, went even further, when he criticized the economic forces that had created the *Titanic* and called for less grandiose shipbuilding:

> For my part I could much sooner believe in an unsinkable ship of 3,000 tons than in one of 40,000 tons. In reading the reports, the first reflection which occurs to one is that, if that luckless ship had been a couple of hundred feet shorter, she would probably have gone clear of the danger. But then, perhaps, she could not have had a swimming bath and a French café. That, of course, is a serious consideration.

> It is inconceivable to think that there are people who can't spend five days of their life without a suite of apartments, cafés, band and such-like refined delights. I suspect that the public is not so very guilty in this matter. These things were pushed on to it in the usual course of trade competition. If to-morrow you were to take all these luxuries away, the public would still travel.

Despite Conrad's warnings, ships did get larger, and luxury remained paramount. But other changes made all passenger liners safer. Shortly after the sinking, shipping lanes were shifted farther south, and all ships carrying fifty or more people were required to have a twenty-four-hour radio watch. Lifeboat drills also became mandatory.

In 1914 representatives of the world's major maritime nations gathered to create the International Ice Patrol. With the exception of the years during the two world wars, this patrol has sighted, marked, and tracked thousands of icebergs. Some years, over a thousand icebergs drift below the 48th parallel, while in others there are none. The ice patrol's record is enviable. No lives have been lost to ice in the area it monitors during its many years of service.

The *Titanic*'s high death toll starkly demonstrated the criminal inanity of existing lifeboat regulations. Soon all ships were required to carry enough lifeboats to hold everyone on board. Immediately following the disaster, manufacturers of lifeboats experienced a surge in demand. Among those who appreciated this was Mrs. Tillie Taussig of New York, who had lost her husband in the sinking. Included in Mr. Taussig's estate were some previously worthless shares of stock in the Engelhardt Collapsible Lifeboat Company. Five months after the *Titanic* tragedy, Mrs. Taussig sold the shares for two thousand dollars, a considerable sum in 1912.

With the advent of World War I, interest in the *Titanic* died away, but even then it seemed that the ship was seldom far from public consciousness. In 1930 the film "Atlantic" appeared — a version of a stage play based upon the sinking. Two years later, Noel Coward's "Cavalcade" reached the screen with its now clichéd scene of two newlyweds who move from where they are standing on deck to reveal a *Titanic* life ring. During World War II, Germany even produced a propaganda film called "Titanic," whose hero was the ship's sole German officer, an invented character.

The 1950s marked the decade of a major *Titanic* reawakening. First came the 1953 Twentieth Century Fox production, "Titanic." Originally titled "Nearer My God to Thee," the story line of this first major motion picture about the disaster dealt with fictional characters and their problems, including an alcoholic former priest played by Richard Basehart, an estranged

A group of Titanic *survivors gathers in Southampton in 1958 for the premiere of the motion picture based on Walter Lord's 1955 bestseller,* A Night to Remember.

The Rank Organization's A Night to Remember *still stands as the most compelling and accurate film account of the disaster.*

couple, played by Clifton Webb and Barbara Stanwyck, struggling for custody of their children, and a young Robert Wagner in love with their daughter, Audrey Dalton.

Next came Walter Lord's 1955 best-selling book *A Night to Remember*. Drawing on interviews with over sixty survivors, the work described the sinking from the moment Frederick Fleet sighted the iceberg until the rescue by the *Carpathia* was complete.

A diver on the set of Raise the Titanic *creates a startling illusion with a fifty-five-foot model of the ship used in the making of the 1980 film based on Clive Cussler's popular novel.*

Suddenly the world was captivated by the disaster all over again. Kraft Television Theater's 1956 production of Lord's book was so popular that it was rerun only five weeks after its original broadcast. Then in 1958 the book was turned into a highly successful documentary-style movie, with Fourth Officer Joseph Boxhall as a technical advisor. Kenneth More played a heroic Second Officer Lightoller.

In recent decades the *Titanic* has appeared on the large screen in the movie *Raise the Titanic*, based on the best-selling book by Clive Cussler. The series premiere of television's "Time Tunnel" was the *Titanic*'s maiden voyage and the sinking figured prominently in the mini-series "Upstairs Downstairs." A lengthy drama was produced in 1979, entitled "S.O.S. Titanic." More often than not this television attention has served to perpetuate myths rather than dispel them.

Today there are many thousands of *Titanic* enthusiasts around the world, including over five thousand members of the Titanic Historical Society, founded in 1963 by Edward S. Kamuda. The T.H.S. publishes a quarterly magazine called the "*Titanic* Commutator" and possesses a small trove of *Titanic* memorabilia, including the model of the ship used in the 1953 movie and the actual lifejacket worn by Madeleine Astor. Every few years conventions are held which draw hundreds of members as well as many of the remaining survivors.

Following the discovery of the wreck in 1985 and the publication of Robert Ballard's international best-seller, *The Discovery of the Titanic*, in 1987, interest in the ship shows no signs of diminishing. Different aspects of the event captivate different people. Most are drawn to the human drama of the story itself. Some are fascinated by the best-documented voyage from the grand era of the luxury liner. Others are lured by the tale of lost innocence, when the technological arrogance of the Edwardians came crashing down. And others still are drawn to the unsolved historical mysteries: Was the *Californian* really the ship seen from the *Titanic*? Did First Officer Murdoch really shoot himself? What music did the band play?

The *Titanic* has become part of our culture and folklore, a part of everyday speech. No other shipwreck can make this claim. No real-life story can match it.

THE *OLYMPIC*: OLD RELIABLE

O f the three giant ships envisioned at Lord Pirrie's dinner party in 1907, only one fulfilled the dream. In contrast with the abbreviated lives of her sisters, the *Titanic* and the *Britannic*, the *Olympic*'s career spanned almost a quarter of a century. Following the *Titanic* disaster, the *Olympic* spent six months at Harland and Wolff undergoing an extensive refit that extended the double bottom up the sides of the vessel to give her a "double skin," and increased her lifeboat capacity. By the spring of 1913 the refurbished liner was back in service on the North Atlantic passenger route.

For several months following the outbreak of war in August of 1914, the *Olympic* remained in commercial service and even rescued the crew of a British battleship that had struck a mine off the coast of Ireland. Commissioned as a naval transport in September, 1915, she spent the rest of the war ferrying soldiers to the front. In wartime "dazzle" paint, the *Olympic* survived four submarine attacks, transported 119,000 civilians and troops, and earned the nickname "Old Reliable."

After a post-war refit, the *Olympic* was back in the sea lanes by July of 1920. Over the next fifteen years, she made hundreds of crossings, most of them routine. One major mishap, however, occurred in heavy fog on May 15, 1934, when she rammed the Nantucket lightship, seven of whose eleven crew members were lost. That same year saw the merger of White Star with Cunard. In March of 1935, losing business to newer ships, the grand old liner made her final New York voyage before being sold, stripped of her fittings, and finally scrapped.

The 1920s were boom years for the Olympic. *(Top) Well-wishers crowd the New York pier as the liner begins another crossing. (Above) The ship's orchestra provides dance music for passengers on B-deck. (Right) In the first-class lounge, gentlemen enjoy a card game while a steward brings them tea. An Art Deco magazine ad from 1933 (far right) celebrates "the gift of gracious living White Star offers."*

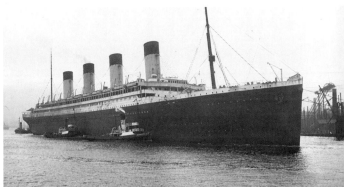

(Left) Brightly painted in geometric shapes to confuse enemy submarines, the Olympic crosses the Atlantic packed with soldiers and lifeboats during World War I.

(Top) The end of a career. The Olympic arrives in the Tyneside town of Jarrow for scrapping.

(Above) Fifty-six years after she was dismantled, carved oak woodwork from the Olympic was found in a barn in northern England and offered for sale.

(Below) Stripped of its superstructure, the Olympic's hull is towed to Inverkeithing, Scotland, for final demolition.

THE UNLUCKY *BRITANNIC*

Work had barely begun on the third and largest of the *Olympic*-class liners when construction was halted to await the outcome of the inquiry into the loss of the *Titanic*. When work resumed, numerous changes (including a name change from *Gigantic* to *Britannic*) were incorporated into the final plans. These included a "double skin" which increased her beam by two feet, watertight bulkheads extending as high as B-deck, and giant-sized lifeboat davits.

The *Britannic* was launched on February 26, 1914, and White Star announced that the new liner would commence service between Southampton and New York in the spring of 1915. But the outbreak of war intervened, and the *Britannic*'s nearly-completed interiors were turned into the dormitories and operating rooms of a hospital ship. On December 12, 1915, she was ready for war service, painted in white with a green stripe and large red crosses on her side.

On a trip from Salonika on November 21, 1916, as she was steaming through the Kea Channel in the Aegean, the *Britannic* was suddenly rocked by a tremendous explosion and quickly began to sink by the bow. Her captain tried in vain to beach her on Kea Island, but within an hour she had gone to the bottom. Of the 1,100 on board only thirty died. Why the *Britannic* sank has never fully been resolved — some claim she was torpedoed although it seems more likely that she struck a mine. Today she lies in 350 feet of water, the largest liner on the ocean floor.

Although White Star denied that the new ship was ever to have been named Gigantic, *this period poster (left) supports the view that the original name is no myth.*

(Above) A booklet celebrating the 1914 launch. (Below) Three views of the Britannic *in service as a hospital ship, showing her large davits that could hold six boats each.*

Underwater exploration of the Britannic wreck (left) by Jacques Cousteau (above) in 1976 revealed that the ship was largely intact save for the massive hole in her forward bow. (Top) A White Star Line cigarette tin saved from the Britannic as she sank.

POSTSCRIPT

WHAT HAPPENED TO THE *TITANIC*'S SURVIVORS IN THE days and years that followed the night the world would never forget? Here is a summary of the post-*Titanic* lives of some of the people featured in our story.

Olaus Abelseth tried vacationing in Canada to calm his nerves following his ordeal on the *Titanic*, but found that simply going back to work was just what he needed. Returning to the South Dakota farm he had first homesteaded in 1908, he raised cattle and sheep for the next thirty years before retiring in North Dakota where he died in 1980.

Madeleine Astor inherited from her husband the income from a five-million-dollar trust fund and the use of his homes on Fifth Avenue and in Newport so long as she did not marry. In August 1912, she gave birth to a son who was named after his father. She relinquished the Astor income and mansions during World War I to marry William K. Dick of New York, and by him had two more sons. She divorced Dick in Reno, Nevada, in 1933 to marry Italian prize-fighter Enzo Fiermonte. Five years later, this marriage also ended in divorce. She died in Palm Beach, Florida, in 1940 at the age of forty-seven.

Nellie Becker and her three children settled in Benton Harbor, Michigan, until her husband's arrival from India the following year. It was apparent to him and their older daughter, Ruth, that Nellie's personality had changed since the disaster. She was far more nervous and was now given to emotional outbursts. Until her death in 1961, she was never able to discuss the *Titanic* disaster without dissolving into tears. Her younger daughter, **Marion Becker,** contracted tuberculosis at a young age and died in Glendale, California, in 1944. **Richard Becker** became a singer and later a social welfare officer. Widowed twice, he passed away in 1975.

Ruth Becker attended high school and college in Ohio, after which she taught high school in Kansas. She married a classmate, Daniel Blanchard, and after their divorce twenty years later, she resumed her teaching career. Like most survivors, she refused to talk about the sinking, and her own children, when young, did not know she had been on the *Titanic*. It was only after her retirement, when she was living in Santa Barbara, California, that she began speaking about it, granting interviews and attending conventions of the Titanic Historical Society. In March of 1990, she made her first sea voyage since 1912, a cruise to Mexico. She passed away later that year at the age of ninety.

Richard and Sallie Beckwith continued to travel, and entertained frequently at their homes in New York City and Squam Lake, New Hampshire. Richard died in New York in 1933 and his wife in that city in 1955.

Karl Behr and Helen Newsom were married in March of 1913, amid sensational newspaper coverage that claimed he had proposed in the lifeboat. He continued to play tennis and, through 1915, was ranked among the top ten players. During his business career, Behr was director of Herman Behr Company, a vice-president of Dillon, Read and Company, and on the board of many corporations including Goodyear Tire and Rubber, and National Cash Register. He was also nominated for the position of governor to the territory of Alaska. After his death in 1949, Helen married Dean Mathey, another tennis player and a good friend of her first husband. She died in New Jersey in 1965.

Joseph Boxhall, the Fourth Officer on the *Titanic*, attained a command with the Royal Navy but was never made captain while in the merchant service. He left the sea in 1940 and in 1958 acted as technical advisor to the film, "A Night to Remember." Following his death in 1967, his ashes were scattered over the ocean in the vicinity of the *Titanic*'s sinking.

Harold Bride kept a very low profile in the years following the disaster. World War I found him as the wireless operator aboard a tiny steamer, the *Mona's Isle*. He later embarked on a career as a salesman before retiring to Scotland where he passed away in April 1956.

Molly Brown's life took a surprising turn after the sinking. While previously, her efforts to be accepted by Denver society had been unsuccessful, the selflessness and heroism she had shown during the disaster prompted her neighbors, for a short time, to open their doors to her. In 1914, she was named as a potential candidate for Congress. As time passed, however, she grew increasingly eccentric. Her husband died intestate and she found herself at odds with her children over his money. In 1932, at the age of sixty-five, she died suddenly in New York City of a stroke. It was only after her death, when she became the subject of the hit Broadway musical and film, "The Unsinkable Molly Brown," that she gained the fame she would have so enjoyed in life.

Kate Buss safely reached San Diego, where she and her fiancé, Samuel Willis, were married on May 11, 1912. Together they raised a daughter, whom they named after Lilian Carter, and after their retirement moved to Pasadena to be closer to her. After Sam's death in 1953, Kate followed her daughter to Oregon where her son-in-law was a minister. She was never able to discuss the *Titanic* disaster without becoming emotional and weeping. She died in Oregon in 1972 at the age of ninety-six.

Selena Cook's husband eventually followed her to the United States and the two settled in Pennsylvania. She was an officer in the Daughters of the King organization and was active in her church and her local historical society. She died in 1964.

Frederick Fleet, the lookout who first sighted the iceberg that sank the *Titanic*, left the sea in 1936. He worked for Harland and Wolff's Southampton shipyard during World War II, after which he became a night watchman for the Union Castle Line. As he moved into old age, he sold newspapers on a street corner in Southampton. In 1965, despondent over his finances and the recent loss of his wife, Fleet took his own life.

Colonel Archibald Gracie became the first serious historian of the *Titanic* disaster, corresponding with other survivors and collecting data for his excellent work, *The Truth About the Titanic*. Regrettably, his book was published posthumously; Colonel Gracie's health declined until he passed away in December of 1912. The second survivor to die, he was preceded by three-year-old **Eugenie Baclini**, a Lebanese immigrant who had succumbed to meningitis the previous August.

Esther Hart and her daughter, Eva, remained in New York only long enough to arrange passage back to England, their hopes of a new life in Canada having died with Benjamin Hart. Esther never remarried, and died of cancer in 1928. After her mother's death, **Eva Hart** moved to Australia and embarked on a singing career. Eventually she returned to England and for many years was an industrial welfare officer and magistrate. She received an MBE for her social work and now lives in retirement outside London. In 1987, she was one of the most outspoken critics of the expedition that recovered artifacts from the wreck of the *Titanic*.

≥ **Robert Hichens**, the quartermaster who had been at the wheel at the time of the *Titanic*'s collision, eventually relocated to South Africa where he became the harbormaster at Cape Town. In the 1920s, he confided to an officer of a ship then in port that the White Star Line had arranged for his move and new career in order to silence him. Hichens' testimony at the inquiries gave no indication that he was hiding anything, and it is more likely that the White Star Line didn't know what to do with the man who had steered the *Titanic* into an iceberg. Sailors were notoriously superstitious, and Hichens, though innocent of any responsibility for the disaster, was probably unwelcome aboard other ships.

≥ **J. Bruce Ismay** retired as planned from the International Mercantile Marine in June 1913, but the position of managing director of the White Star Line that he had hoped to retain was denied him. Surviving the *Titanic* disaster had made him far too unpopular with the public. He spent his remaining years alternating between his homes in London and Ireland. Because Ismay had never had many close friends, and subsequently had few business contacts, it was mistakenly assumed that he had become a recluse. He did enjoy being kept informed of shipping news but those around him were forbidden to mention the *Titanic*. He died in 1937.

≥ **Marie Jerwan** suffered from nightmares and panic attacks for weeks following the disaster. Eventually she recovered, but her later years were plagued with misfortune. She battled cancer for decades, was seriously injured in a car accident and, in 1974, at the age of eighty-six, died soon after breaking her hip.

≥ **Charles H. Lightoller**, the *Titanic*'s senior surviving officer, did his best to protect his employers at the two official inquiries that followed the shipwreck but later found his career blocked by the disaster. The command of any of the White Star vessels seemed to elude him, and it was only during World War I, while serving with the Royal Navy, that he was made a commander. After the war he found work ashore for several years before opening his own guesthouse and ultimately becoming a successful chicken farmer. During World War II he used his private yacht, the *Sundowner*, to assist in the evacuation at Dunkirk. He passed away in December 1952.

≥ **Harold Lowe**, like other officers of the *Titanic*, never became a captain while in the merchant service but attained the rank of commander while serving in the Royal Naval Reserve during World War I. He eventually left the sea and returned to his home in North Wales where he became very active civically and sat on the local town council. He died in 1944.

≥ After returning to France with his mother and brother, **Edmond Navratil** grew up, married, and embarked on a career as an interior decorator, later becoming an architect and builder. He served in the French Army during World War II, and was imprisoned in a German prisoner-of-war camp. He escaped, but his health did not recover from the ordeal, and he died at the age of forty-three. **Michel Navratil** married a fellow student in 1933 while studying philosophy at a university. He eventually earned his doctorate and became a professor of psychology. In 1987, for the seventy-fifth anniversary of the disaster, he returned to the United States for the first time since 1912, to attend a reunion of survivors arranged by the Titanic Historical Society. He now lives in retirement in France.

≥ Rumors circulated in Canadian military circles that **Major Arthur Peuchen** would not be receiving a promotion to Lieutenant-Colonel of the Queen's Own Rifles, an advancement which had been practically assured before the disaster. On May 21, 1912, the promotion was indeed given, but within a few years the stigma which followed many of the male survivors — of having lived when so many men had died — caused him to leave Ontario and eventually settle in Alberta. He died there in 1929.

≥ **Herbert Pitman** remained at sea for thirty-five more years, although failing vision forced him to leave the bridge and join the purser's staff. For a period, he even found himself serving aboard the *Olympic*. A widower, he retired to the town of Pitcombe, England, where he lived with a niece until his death in December 1961.

≥ After her arrival in New York, **Emily Ryerson** attended funeral services for her son and her husband. During the First World War, she assisted Herbert Hoover in working for the American Fund for the French Wounded, for which she received the Croix de Guerre. She divided her time between her home in Chicago and the family summer home in Cooperstown, New York, and also made frequent trips abroad. In Peking she met Forsythe Sherfesee, a financial advisor to the Chinese Government, and the two were married in 1927. She left Chicago for a house in Cap Ferrat, France, and died in 1939 while vacationing in Montevideo, Uruguay.

≥ **Elmer and Juliet Taylor** returned to the United States in 1914 to live but continued to cross the Atlantic frequently, often on the *Olympic*. Mrs. Taylor died suddenly in April 1927, and her husband remarried twice before passing away in 1949. By the time of his death, he had crossed the Atlantic sixty times.

≥ **Marian Thayer** never remarried following the *Titanic* disaster, and lived out her life in Haverford, Pennsylvania. She died on April 14, 1944. Her son, **Jack Thayer**, graduated from the University of Pennsylvania and went into banking, later returning to his alma mater as treasurer and financial vice-president. Throughout his life he was haunted by the memory of the *Titanic* sinking and in 1945, despondent over the death of a son in the war, he took his own life.

≥ **Edwina Troutt** suffered emotionally for months following the sinking. In 1916 she moved to Southern California to escape the eastern winters, married a baker, and settled in Beverly Hills. Eventually she put the *Titanic* experience behind her and for forty years rarely mentioned it. She ultimately outlived three husbands during forty-seven years of retirement in Hermosa Beach, California. Often interviewed about her experiences, she became a celebrity as a *Titanic* survivor. In Hermosa Beach, however, she was better known for her many civic activities. She died in 1984, five months after her 100th birthday.

≥ **Eleanor Widener** devoted much of the rest of her life to extensive charitable works, the most notable of which was the Harry Elkins Widener Memorial Library which she built for Harvard University. In 1915 she married Dr. Alexander Hamilton Rice of New York City, a noted geographer and explorer, and with him embarked on several South American expeditions. She and her husband also traveled extensively in Europe and India. She passed away in Paris in 1937.

≥ **R. Norris Williams**, along with a handful of other European survivors, took the return maiden voyage of the *France* home in May, 1912. He went back to America several months later to enter Harvard and continue his tennis career. By the end of the year, he was ranked second in the United States and by the mid-1920s, had twice won the National Amateur Singles tennis championship and twice the U.S. Doubles championship. After World War I, in which he was awarded the Croix de Guerre and the Legion of Honor from France, he embarked on a career as an investment banker. For twenty-two years he was a director of the Philadelphia Historical Society, retiring only a few years before his death in 1968.

≥ **Marion Wright** and her fiancé, Arthur Woolcott, were married in New York at St. Christopher's Chapel on April 20. The following day they headed west to Cottage Grove, Oregon, where they raised three sons. Marion never liked to speak of the *Titanic* but would do so on the anniversary of the sinking for those friends or family who were interested. Arthur died in 1961, and Marion in 1965.

Index

Design, Typography and Art Direction
GORDON SIBLEY DESIGN INC.

Editorial Director
HUGH BREWSTER

Editorial Assistance
RICK ARCHBOLD, SHELLEY TANAKA, CATHERINE FRACCARO,
IAN R. COUTTS, WANDA NOWAKOWSKA

Production Director
SUSAN BARRABLE

Production Assistance
DONNA CHONG

Maps and Diagrams
PETER KOVALIK

Printing and Binding
IMAGO PRODUCTIONS (F.E.) LTD., SINGAPORE

TITANIC: AN ILLUSTRATED HISTORY
was produced by Madison Press Books